The Life of Chief Joseph

Alan E. Grey

University of Nebraska Press
Lincoln and London

First Nebraska paperback printing: 2014

Library of Congress Cataloging-in-Publication Data
Grey, Alan E.
The life of Chief Joseph / Alan E. Grey.
pages   cm
Originally published: Idaho Falls, Ida.: Wasatch Press, c2008.
Includes bibliographical references.
ISBN 978-0-8032-6934-7 (pbk.: alk. paper) 1. Joseph, Nez Percé Chief, 1840–
1904. 2. Nez Percé Indians—Biography. 3. Nez Percé Indians—Wars, 1877.
4. Nez Percé Indians—History. I. Title.
E99.N5 J5832
979.0049741240092—dc23
[B]
2014001702

ACKNOWLEDGMENTS

One of the objectives of this book was to keep it as historically and culturally accurate as possible, yet write in a manner that will hold the interest of the younger readers. In order to achieve these objectives, I had the help of many different sources.

I am particularly indebted to Mr. Robert Applegate, Research Center Manager, Nez Perce National Historical Park, Lapwai, Idaho, who provided me with valuable information and directed me to additional sources of information at the Historical Park.

I would also like to thank Mr. Jim Kittle who is a Journalism Instructor at Hillcrest High School in Idaho Falls, Idaho. Jim did a final editing job on my manuscript, and gave invaluable assistance in finding my current publisher.

Last but far from least, I want to thank my wife Lois, who did an initial review for typographical errors and who endured the many hours I spent in isolation at the computer.

TABLE OF CONTENTS

Chapter 1

Start of the Nez Perce Discontent

During the middle of April, 1845, a wagon train consisting of forty-one wagons left Independence, Missouri for the long trip over the Oregon Trail to the new Oregon Territory. One of the men making this westward trek was Joel Palmer. Joel Palmer had been elected to the Indiana Legislature the previous year, but the lure of adventure was calling him west. Based on his leadership ability, he was elected wagon-train captain by his fellow travelers.[1]

The Oregon Trail was opened in 1841, when a small wagon train consisting of sixty-nine people made their way from Independence, Missouri to the Oregon territory. The traffic over the trail increased each year, hitting its peak in 1849, when some 55,000 people made the crossing. From 1841 through 1850, it is estimated that approximately 125,000 emigrants made the trip west.[2]

Many of the emigrants settled in the Willamette Valley of Oregon, while others explored the Columbia Plateau region of Eastern Washington and Oregon as possible locations for farms and ranches. This area contained the ancestral homes of the Wallowa Nez Perce and several related tribes. The influx of settlers onto the tribal lands was an increasing source of irritation and conflict between the settlers and the Indian people.

Late in the summer of 1853, another cause of concern arose. Rumors started flying that Lt. George B. McClelland and a small group of soldiers were mapping a route through the Indian land for the railroad. Some of the soldiers were also telling the Indians they met that a man more important than McClelland, named Stevens, was on his way from the East to become Governor of the Washington Territory and was to take over whatever lands the white men needed.

Another important event of 1853 was Oregon splitting away from the Washington Territory. Shortly thereafter, Joel Palmer was appointed Superintendent of Indian Affairs for the Oregon Territory. After this separation, the Washington Territory covered the area which now forms the state of Washington, part of Northern Idaho, and a portion of Montana. When Isaac Stevens arrived in Olympia, Washington, he became Governor and Superintendent of Indian Affairs for that Territory.[3] The aforementioned events were the basis for many council meetings among the Indian tribes. Their primary concern was how to meet this threat. Should they try to negotiate a peaceful settlement with the white man, or should they meet this invasion with war? These problems were of particular concern for Old Chief Joseph whose ancestral home was the Wallowa Valley of Eastern Oregon.

During early April of 1855, the rumors became a reality. James Doty, Governor Stevens' Secretary, and Andrew J. Bolon, who had been appointed by Stevens as his sub-chief for all tribes living in Washington east of the Cascades, came to the Lapwai mission to arrange a council. The council was to be held on May 29, 1855, at the traditional meeting place in the Walla Walla Valley, close to the ruins of the Whitman Mission. Governor Stevens' envoy tried to impress the assembled Nez Perce with how grand the Council would be. The Nez Perce were told that the other related tribes in the area had agreed to attend. In addition, both Governor Stevens and Joel Palmer would be in attendance. Most of the Nez Perce had met Joel Palmer, and they liked and trusted him. James Doty and Andrew Bolin finished their presentation by stating that the Council would not succeed if the Nez Perce did not attend, since they were by far the largest tribe in the area.[4]

Old Chief Joseph and the other Nez Perce Chiefs held many councils debating what the white man was going to demand and what they should do if some of these demands occurred.

Old Chief Joseph was convinced that the white man's superiority was the result of his religion. He and his people had spent many years around the Lapwai Mission trying to learn as much as possible about the white man's religion. Old Chief Joseph felt that this religion would protect him and his people from any unjust demands the white leaders might make at the upcoming council meeting at Walla Walla.

Shortly after James Doty and Andrew Bolon obtained assurance that the Nez Perce would attend the council meeting, they left to report back to Governor Stevens. The head chiefs of the various Nez Perce groups returned to their traditional winter campgrounds along the Clearwater and Salmon Rivers to inform their people what had happened and to prepare for the trip to the council meeting at Walla Walla.

Old Chief Joseph and his group stayed at Lapwai making preparations to leave for Walla Walla, some 120 miles to the West, in ample time to arrive a few days prior to the council meeting. Old Chief Joseph had brought his entire group to the Lapwai Mission, including old men, warriors, women and children, along with all of their horses. This group included Old Chief Joseph's two sons, Young Joseph and Ollikut.

Young Joseph was just entering his fifteenth year, considered by most tribes as the start of manhood. His brother Ollikut was probably two years younger. Young Joseph had been baptized shortly after his birth and had been given the name Joseph. He and his father now had the same name which caused some confusion. To keep the two straight, they were known as Old Joseph and Young Joseph.

While some claim the contrary, there is no record that Ollikut was ever baptized. Thus, he retained his Indian name which means "Frog."[5]

Chapter 2

Trip to Walla Walla

The trees and meadows along the Clearwater River were still in deep shadows. The sun had not yet risen over the mountains when Joseph and his brother Ollikut came out of their parents' tepee. They jumped on their horses that had been hobbled close to the tepee the night before. Joseph, the first to mount, called to his brother, "Hurry Ollikut, we must get father's horses rounded up by dawn as we have a long trip ahead of us."

When Joseph and Ollikut arrived at the lower meadow, some of the other Nez Perce boys were already there. "Yo, Him mah too yah lat kekht!"

shouted one of the boys. This was Joseph's Nez Perce name which meant "Thunder Rolling in the Mountains." Joseph preferred his Indian name, the one he had found while on his vision quest three years before, when he was twelve. This name had religious and tribal significance that he did not feel with the name Joseph. (Only the person with the name knew for certain the dream or vision from which the name came.)

In a short time the boys had rounded up all of the horses and headed back toward the main encampment. The women had already taken down the tepees and were finishing the packing of the family belongings. Young Joseph and Ollikut were happy that their mother had a hearty breakfast of hot grain cereal waiting for them.

The head men of the tribe were seated around a campfire debating what the white chiefs were going to demand and how far the tribe would go to meet those demands. Old Chief Joseph was primarily worried about the Wallowa Valley area of the Oregon Territory where they and their ancestors had lived since the beginning of time. All of their ancestors were buried there, and the land was sacred to them.

By midmorning, Old Chief Joseph and the rest of his people were ready to start their trip to Walla Walla. Young Joseph, Ollikut, and the other horse herders started first. They were responsible for a large herd of some of the finest horses in the Northwest. The Nez Perce, well known for their horse-breeding ability, were very proud of the animals they owned. Because these horses were found in the Palouse area of the Northwest they were known as Palouse Horses. Due to the slurred pronunciation of the white settlers, they finally became know as Appaloosa Horses. Most of the horses had the characteristic dapple gray area on their flank and each family counted its wealth by the number of horses it owned.[1]

The horse herd was strung out for about a half mile as the young herders guided them along the banks of the Clearwater River. Behind the horse herd came the tribal elders and warriors, followed by the women and children and supplies needed for the trip. Joseph and Ollikut were content. The sun was warm on their backs, and the sounds of the Clearwater River could easily be heard as they rode along the bank.

By noon they were on the banks of the Snake River just upstream from where it merged with the

Clearwater River, close to the present city of Lewiston, Idaho. With whoops and much yelling, the boys drove the horses into the river and started the long swim across to the opposite shore. About an hour later, the horses were all on the other side. The boys were excitedly congratulating each other that none of the horses had been lost during the crossing. Soon the tribal elders had crossed and the women and children were just starting.

Nez Perce children were taught to ride almost as soon as they could walk; therefore, some of the children were able to ride their horses across the Snake River. Each very young child was either tied to the horse in front of his mother or in a carrier basket attached to his mother's back. As soon as everyone was safely across, they started up the trail out of the Snake River canyon. It was about a mile climb out of the canyon: a long steep trail with many switchbacks. Upon reaching the top, the horses were turned west across the rolling hills of the Inland Empire toward their destination of Walla Walla.

Young Joseph and Ollikut were riding together, off to the side of the horse herd to stay out of the dust. There were a few puffy white clouds in a clear blue sky. The hills in the middle of May were still green and would not turn the brown of summer for another month or so. Across the fields they could see the young camas plants just coming into bloom with their delicate light blue flowers. The Blue Mountains shimmered in the far distance. Joseph turned to his brother and said, "Ollikut, if heaven is as Reverend Spalding tells us, it must be something like this." Ollikut thought for a while and replied, "Yes Joseph, you must be right, but if I have my choice, I will stay right here." The two boys rode on in silence, deep in their own thoughts.

The tribal elders had selected a spot on Asotin Creek, a little to the south and west of their present location, for the first night camp site. By late afternoon they had all arrived. Asotin Creek, a small stream fed by mountain snow, flows into the Snake River about ten miles upstream from where Chief Joseph and his people had crossed. The stream, lined with willow thickets and brush, had many deep holes filled with trout.

After arriving at the camp, the first job of the herders was to take care of the horses. They were watered well downstream of the camp to keep the water near the camp from being muddied. After they

Reverend Henry H. Spalding
(Dept. of Interior, Nez Perce National Historical Park)

were watered, the herd was driven to a large field where the horses could graze. Two boys had to stay with the herd to see that they did not wander off or were driven off by any hostile Indian band passing through the area. Each set of boys had to stay with the herd for about two hours. Young Joseph and Ollikut had chosen from four to six in the morning, when the sun was just coming up. This was their favorite time of day.

By the time the horses were watered, the women had already set up camp. They did not put up the tepees, as the weather was too balmy and there was no threat of rain. Young Joseph and Ollikut were looking forward to sleeping under the stars. Each had his own buffalo robe, so there was no chance of getting cold.

The boys not tending horses were now free to do as they pleased. Many of them wanted to practice with their bows and arrows. Some just wanted to shoot at targets to improve their skill, while others went out hunting for rabbits, hoping to bring some fresh meat to their families. Young Joseph and Ollikut decided to try their luck at fishing. They got the fishing spears their father had made for them and started up Asotin Creek, looking for some promising holes to try their luck. About a half mile up the stream there was a large boulder right at the edge of the water with a deep hole on the downstream side. Peeking over the top of the bolder, they saw the hole was filled with many large trout.

Young Joseph was the first to try his luck. Carefully easing himself onto the boulder, he inched forward, taking care not to scare the fish by brushing pebbles or other debris into the water. He also made certain not to cast a shadow on the water as this would also disturb the fish. Young Joseph lay quietly watching the pool. He soon saw a large trout rise to the surface after a bug that had dropped into the water. With a smooth easy motion he thrust the spear into the trout and flipped it up onto the bank. Backing off of the boulder he said, "Ollikut, there is the first fish. Now it is your turn to try your luck."

It took a little while for the fish to settle down and return to their feeding. Fifteen minutes later, Ollikut had speared his first fish. After each catch, it took longer for the fish to return to the pool.

About two hours later, Young Joseph and Ollikut returned to their parents' campfire with four large trout. When their mother saw the trout she was very pleased and said, "You are both good fishermen. Your father has taught you well." She took the trout a short distance from camp and soon had them cleaned and ready for cooking. While cleaning the fish, she sent Ollikut to the creek for four willow branches. He removed the small twigs and bark and sharpened one end. Their mother took the four willow branches and secured a trout to each one by thrusting the branch through the mouth and out the back by the tail. She then placed them over a willow frame she had made on each side of the fire, and occasionally rotated the fish so they would cook evenly on all sides. The frame would not burn as it was made of green willow and out of the direct flame of the fire.

Soon Chief Joseph came and exclaimed, "Where did these fish come from?" His wife quietly explained how the boys had gotten them from the creek. It was not the Indian way to show much emotion, but a smile from their father let the boys know that he was well pleased.

After dinner, there was not a bit of meat left on the bones of the fish. Their mother then gave them each a piece of pemmican. This high-energy food used by the Nez Perce as well as most other Indian tribes, was made by pounding venison into a paste, then adding fat, dried and powdered camas root, and berries. This was well mixed and then divided into small cakes which were dried.

As the sun disappeared in the west, the whole encampment settled down for the night. As the boys settled into their robes, they tried to identify the various sounds they heard. The howling of coyotes and the hooting of owls were easy to recognize, but the twitter of some of the night birds and the chirp of small animals were much more difficult. Soon Young Joseph said, "Brother, we must get some sleep as we will be called for our duty as horse tenders much sooner than we would like."

It seemed they had just fallen asleep when they were called to go. When they arose, they rolled and tied their buffalo robes and stacked them by the family gear. As usual, their horses were hobbled close to their camp. They soon had the hobble ropes removed from the front legs and a rope halter put on the horses. Both boys rode bare-back so they were soon on their way out to the herd. The two boys they were relieving were very happy to see them coming.

When they arrived at the horse herd, the world was still shrouded in pre-dawn darkness. In a short time a soft golden glow was emerging in the east. As the sun rose higher, the surrounding hill came into view. The grass, covered with early morning dew, sparkled like a field full of diamonds. A cool breeze from the west carried the melodious sound of meadow larks and killdeers greeting the morning with their songs.

For the next two hours, Young Joseph and Ollikut rode slowly around the herd. Most of the horses were already stirring and starting to graze. Each boy was deep in his own thoughts, content with the world and looking forward to the day ahead.

As the dawn was breaking, the women arose and started their cooking fires. It wasn't long before the rest of the camp began to stir. Soon the boys became hungered by the aroma of breakfast cooking over the various campfires. Young Joseph and Ollikut were both happy when they saw their replacements.

It took very little time for the women to perform the routine of cleaning up after breakfast and packing the family gear. By the time the sun was full in the sky, everyone was ready to travel. For the rest of the day, the Nez Perce group traveled up Asotin Creek, making camp that night near the headwaters. In the early afternoon of the fourth day, Chief Joseph and his people arrived at the Walla Walla Council site.

Chapter 3

The Treaty of 1855

On arrival at the Walla Walla council area, Chief Joseph and his group chose a campsite in a large grassy meadow along Mill Creek, a small tributary of the Walla Walla River. This was approximately one mile from where the Council would be held.[1]

Soon all of the Nez Perce groups to attend the council had arrived, including the head chief and negotiator Hal-hal-tios-sot, also known as Lawyer. Other Nez Perce sub-chiefs present were Looking Glass (the elder) whose Nez Perce name was Ippakness Wayhayken; Spotted Eagle; Joseph (the elder), whose Nez Perce name was Tu-ela-kas; James; Red Wolf;

Chief Lawyer
(Dept. of Interior, Nez Perce National Historical Park)

Timothy; and Eagle-from-the-Light. Chief White Bird, whose Nez Perce name was Peopeo Kisklok Hihih, meaning White Goose, did not attend. His only desire was for peace, but he had a strong distrust of the white men. It is easy to see why the white men preferred the English names. They could hardly pronounce, let alone remember, the Nez Perce names. However, the Nez Perce still preferred to call each other by their Indian names and responded to the English names only out of necessity.[2]

While Chief Lawyer was considered the primary spokesman for the Nez Perce, this position did not meet with full acceptance from all of the sub-chiefs. The distrust of Chief Lawyer stemmed from an incident several years earlier. A Nez Perce chief, given the English name of Ellis, had been looked upon as spokesman for all of the Nez Perce people. Upon his death some of the minor chiefs, including Old Chief Joseph, wanted to be named and elevated to that position. However, Chief Lawyer wasted no time in working his wiles on the white leaders at the Indian Headquarters at Lapwai and was given the position of spokesman. This raised a certain amount of envy among the lesser chiefs, and distrust of Lawyer became a favorite pastime.[3]

In addition to the Nez Perce, other tribes attending the Council meeting were the Umatilla, Walla Walla, Yakima, and Cayuse tribes. In total, it is estimated that more than 5,000 Indians were at the Council meeting.[4]

After all of the Nez Perce bands that were coming to the Council had gathered, they made their grand entrance. An American flag that had been presented to the Nez Perce by Lewis and Clark was taken to the white compound. As soon as the flag was raised, the Nez Perce Chiefs rode slowly toward Stevens and Palmer and were presented in the order of their importance. As soon as the presentations were complete, approximately six hundred mounted warriors charged forward, stopping abruptly in front of the two white negotiators. Forming a ring around the flag pole, a couple dozen warriors jumped off their horses and started dancing. The rest remained mounted, beating out the rhythm on small drums. When the dance was finished, the Nez Perce retired to their campground.[5]

While the opening ceremony was taking place, the women and young girls began setting up tepees and making a permanent camp. They were anxious to finish their work so they could visit old friends they had not seen for many months.

While the women were setting up the camp, the young horse herders were taking care of their herd, making sure the horses were watered and then placed in an adjacent field where they could graze. As soon as the horses were secure, the boys were free to roam about the camp. They were anxious to meet old friends and make new ones. They were soon making plans to show off their various skills at racing and shooting. Ollikut, more athletic than Young Joseph, was very excited about the planned contests. He soon decided on the race he wanted to enter but would bide his time until the proper moment to make the challenge. On the other hand, Young Joseph, more serious, had greater interest in the organization and execution of the various contests.

Actual Council business did not get underway until May 29, 1855. The morning promised to be a beautiful day. The sun was just starting to rise over the hills to the East. A slight cool breeze stirred the morning air, and not a cloud could be seen in the sky.

The tribal chiefs had gathered at the Nez Perce encampment, dressed in their finest buckskin pants and tunics ornately decorated with porcupine quills and colorful beads. Each wife took care and pride in designing patterns to show significant events in her husband's life. In addition to these clothes, many of the chiefs wore their ceremonial head pieces of eagle feathers and white ermine fur. When they had all gathered, they started walking solemnly toward the White Man's Council. The chiefs were followed by several hundred sub-chiefs and curious onlookers.

When they arrived at the council table, the white leaders were already seated. At the center of the table was Isaac Stevens, Governor of the Washington Territory and Superintendent of Indian Affairs. Next to him was Joel Palmer, Oregon Superintendent of Indian Affairs. In addition to these two, there was the usual assortment of military personnel and civilian clerks. The clerks were there to keep a record of all treaty discussions.

Chief Lawyer was the first to approach the white council. In a loud clear voice he said, "I, and my fellow chiefs of the Nez Perce people and principal chiefs of the Cayuse, Walla Walla, Umatilla and Yakima people, have assembled to hear and discuss the plans that you wish to present to us." Concluding these remarks, he introduced himself to Stevens and Palmer. There was no shaking of hands, only a solemn nod toward each other. When this was complete, Chief Lawyer presented each major chief who stepped forward and nodded to the white leaders. When the introductions were complete, Governor Stevens rose and said, "We are honored to be in the presence of such noble men. We hope you will hear and accept the plan we are about to present. I will now let Superintendent Palmer present our plan to you."

When Superintendent Palmer arose and started reading from a sheaf of papers, there was an immediate outcry from the assembled chiefs. Chief Lawyer arose and said, "My brothers the Nez Perce, Walla Walla, Umatilla, Cayuse and Yakima do not understand English as well as you. We want your ideas given to us one at a time. We can then change what you say to our language and understand what you mean." With these words, Chief Lawyer took his seat on the spread blanket and waited for Superintendent Palmer to resume.

Superintendent Palmer again rose and briefly described the purpose of the Council. Each tribe had brought an interpreter who could speak both the white man's language and his own tribal tongue.

Each interpreter told his chief and the assembled people of his own tribe what the white man had said. After all of the chiefs had heard and understood what had been said, they were given time to comment or voice their opinions. The white leaders were dismayed, for the Council was obviously going to last much longer than they had anticipated.[6]

By noon everyone was getting restless. The sun was directly overhead, and all of the people were getting hot and tired. When Governor Stevens saw that everyone was getting restless and losing interest, he called the meeting to an end. He told the assembled chiefs that they would meet again at the same time the next morning. It took a little over two weeks for Superintendent Palmer to explain all of the conditions of the treaty and the boundaries to be established for each tribal reservation.

Each afternoon the chiefs were free to discuss among themselves what they had heard that morning. During this time they could also make plans for arguments they wished to present to the council the next morning. The rest of the afternoon was spent visiting with old friends, dancing, or watching the different contests of skill arranged by the young men of the different tribes. If a young man felt he was the fastest runner, he would stand and challenge all other youths to a race. These challenges would be followed by friendly arguments on the distance to be run and the course to be followed. They would then select older warriors to stand along the race route to see that none of the runners took short cuts. The foot races, horse races, and shooting with both bow and arrows and rifles were the most popular contests.

Ollikut, proud of his Appaloosa pony, rose and said, "I have the fastest horse of anyone here. I will challenge anyone to a horse race of not less than five miles over any type of land you may pick." After a pause he added, "Those who wish to race will tell my brother Joseph no later than tomorrow afternoon. He will select a group of elders to lay out the course we are to follow."

As every youth was equally proud of his horse, it soon became evident that this was going to be a big race. Young Joseph took the names of over fifty young men who wanted to enter. Knowing how important this race was going to be, he consulted his father on how best to handle the details. He wanted the race to be completely fair, to avoid any thought that it was arranged to favor his brother.

Old Joseph looked at his son and said, "You have much responsibility. I can see you are trying to be fair to all who enter the race. You should choose a trusted warrior from each tribe to help arrange the time and lay out the course."

While the various contests were being set up, the women and young girls put on dances of religious and tribal significance. Some of the older youths watched these dances closely. They enjoyed watching the young girls and hoped that they in turn would be noticed by the dancers. The dances and contests of skill were equally enjoyed by the older tribal members and by the white leaders and soldiers who had come to the Council.

A major problem with any gathering of this size was keeping everyone fed. Fortunately, the snow was still deep in the Blue Mountains south of the Council site, so game was still plentiful in the meadows along the river. In addition, the river was beginning to fill with salmon on their spring run upriver. By noon, the hunters would start returning with the game they had killed. This was usually a deer, but occasionally they brought back an antelope or an elk. The game was shared by all families of the tribe.

Every night was a time for the families of all the tribe to gather for celebration and eating. Each woman tried to prepare the finest meal, seasoning the roasts with her own secret blend of leaves and roots she had gathered that morning. The feast celebrations would last well into the evening hours.

Preparations for the contests of skill progressed at a rapid pace. On the afternoon of the fourth day the contests began. The first was skill with the bow and arrow. Eagle Tail, a young Yakima boy, had made the challenge which had been accepted by twenty or so other boys. A small wooden post was set up out in the meadow. A tribal elder then stepped off twenty paces and drew a line in the dirt. Each boy was allowed three arrows and instructed to stand behind the line when shooting. For the first round they could only shoot one arrow. After each shot there was an uproar, either shouts of joy or hooting, depending on whether or not the arrows found the target. At the end of the first round there were eight arrows in the post. Each boy identified his arrow by the markings he had placed on it. The second round was only for the eight boys who had hit the target. At the end of the second round, there were just two arrows in the post; one belonged to Eagle Tail and the other to Spotted Horse, a Walla Walla youth. These two prepared for their third shot. Eagle Tail was the first to shoot; again his arrow found the target. Spotted Horse took careful aim and let his arrow go. The point of the arrow grazed the side of the post and glanced off. Eagle Tail, declared the winner, came over to Spotted Horse and put his arm on his shoulder. He said, "Spotted Horse, you are a good shot. We would do well hunting together; maybe some day we can."

The next day's contest, the rifle shoot for the older boys, was conducted in the same manner as that for the bow and arrow. A white rock was placed out in the field. One of the tribal elders stepped off 100 paces and drew a line in the dirt. Each boy was allowed three bullets and told to stand behind the line. In order to see the rock, partially hidden by the grass, all shots had to be taken from a standing position. The rifles the boys owned were not particularly accurate. They could all hit a deer or elk at one hundred paces, but a small half-hidden rock was a much harder target. Of the fifteen boys in the contest, just three had hit the target after the first round. At the end of the second round, only one shooter had again hit the target. That shooter and winner of the contest was Gray Eagle, a young Nez Perce warrior from Chief Looking Glass's band. That night a victory celebration was held in his honor.

Between these contests there were lesser contests for the younger boys, such as foot races across the field and back to the starting point. These races were watched with as much interest and enthusiasm as was shown for the older boys' contests.

By the sixth day, all preparations were complete for the long-awaited foot race. The course, about two miles long, started in the meadow and headed up over some hills just to the north. At the bank of the Walla Walla River, it turned back south and ended at the starting point. Tribal elders stood about five-hundred yards apart along the race route to see that all runners stayed on the course.

Just over thirty runners entered the race. A warrior seated on a horse had been chosen to start the race. When he fired his rifle in the air all runners took off. Some of the boys started running as fast as they could to get a good head start. However, by the time they reached the first hill, they were out of breath and had to drop to the rear of the race. After about ten minutes, the crowd at the finish line could see some of the runners coming over the last hill. Four runners were very close together. At the edge of the field, Running Deer, a young Walla Walla warrior, broke free and sprinted to the finish line. He won the race by a few steps over the other three.

After eight days, all details for the horse race were finalized. Joseph and seven tribal elders rode around the course, setting up stakes with flags about every quarter of a mile. The course, about five miles long, was full of hazards. There were steep hills to go up and down, plus the Walla Walla River had to be crossed twice. One older warrior would be stationed at each flag to make sure no short cuts were taken.

At noon the next day, the starting shot was fired, and the riders were off. With much whooping and yelling, they raced out of the meadow toward the first flag post. In a short time all riders were out of sight over the hill. Ollikut had started in the middle of the pack and was slowly working his way to the front. Though he was gaining ground on the others, it was not yet time to push his horse. He wanted some of his horse's energy left for a final burst of speed. When he reached the Walla Walla River, there were five horses ahead of him, and one had already reached the other side.

In the middle of the river, one of the horses ahead of Ollikut panicked and threw his rider when he saw a log floating down toward him. Though both the rider and his horse managed to reach shore safely, they had lost too much ground to continue the race. On top of the next hill was the flag to turn toward home.

Ollikut was now within twenty yards of the lead horse. Upon reaching the Walla Walla River, all four riders were bunched together and were still together when they reached the far side. Ollikut knew it was now time to let his horse go into a dead run. He tapped the horse on the right flank with a small quirt that he carried. The horse responded with a sudden burst of speed. When the other riders saw what was happening, they tried to whip their horses into a faster speed, but they did not have the endurance of Ollikut's Appaloosa. Ollikut thundered across the finish line four lengths ahead of his closest rival.

Old Chief Joseph heard all details of the race from the warriors that had been stationed along the race route. That night during the victory celebration, Chief Joseph rose and said, "My son, Ollikut, will be a great warrior. He showed courage and wisdom during the race. He has made me very proud."

The tribes were beginning to get restless and anxious for the Council to end so they could return home. It took about two weeks for the treaty to be read, understood, and for comments to be made on it. At the end of the Council, the Nez Perce seemed well satisfied with the land that had been allotted to them. The smaller tribes were not as happy with the land area and locations where they were told to move. However, because of pressure from the white negotiators and the Nez Perce, they agreed to sign the treaty.

The Nez Perce had been assigned a little over three million acres. This area included land on the north side of the Snake River, both the Clearwater and Salmon River valleys to the east of the Snake River, as well as the lower Grand Ronde, Wallowa and Imnaha valleys west of the Snake River. The one clause of the treaty that seemed to please all of the Indian tribes was that no white man could enter their land without first obtaining their permission. All of the principal chiefs signed the treaty and then made preparations to return to their home territory.[7]

Chapter 4

Years of Turmoil

The day following the treaty signing, Chief Joseph's band packed their belongings and headed for their home territory in the Wallowa Valley, about 120 miles southeast of the Walla Walla Council site.

Young Joseph and Ollikut were again assigned to the group of horse herders. They both knew this trip would be much harder than the one from Lapwai to Walla Walla. Instead of rolling hills, they would be crossing some of the more rugged portions of the Blue Mountains. There would also be rivers to cross, including the Grand Ronde, which were now at flood stage from the spring run-off.

None of the young herders seemed concerned about the trip. They were all talking and laughing about different things that had happened at the council. Gray Eagle, traveling with Joseph's people, was carrying the rifle he had used to win the shooting contest. He would not let the rifle out of his sight and was telling everyone how he took care of the rifle so that it would shoot straight. Ollikut, equally excited, said to everyone that would listen, "We, the Nez Perce, have the finest and fastest horses in the territory. Did I not show that when I won the race?" After a moment's thought he added, "Other tribes want to steal our horses so they too can have these fine animals. We must be ever alert to guard our horses from being stolen."

All that day they traveled in a southeast direction. By that night, they had covered about thirty miles and made camp along the banks of the Walla Walla River. The weather was still warm enough that they could sleep under the stars. However, when the boys arose the next morning, they could see storm clouds gathering in the west.

Shortly after sunup, the trip to the Wallowa Valley resumed. By that night they were well into the Blue Mountains. Chief Joseph and his band made camp in an alpine meadow bordered by a small stream. The storm clouds were now overhead, and flakes of snow were beginning to fall. The women quickly erected windbreaks and sent the young girls out for dry twigs and limbs to build the fires. The evening meal consisted of elk and venison jerky.

The next morning the snow had stopped, but there was over an inch of new snow on the ground. All sounds were muffled by the snow with the exception of a pack of coyotes howling on a nearby hill. In a short time the sun arose; the storm clouds had drifted to the east and the air was crisp and clear. Joseph and Ollikut made a game of identifying the animal tracks they found in the new snow. The most common were those of rabbits. They also identified the tracks of deer and those of a porcupine where it had wandered across the meadow.

Three days later they came to the Wallowa Valley. The name Wallowa is usually defined as the Valley of Winding Waters. It is a high valley, guarded by the Blue Mountains to the south and west, by the canyons of the Grand Ronde River to the north, and by the canyon of the Snake River to the east. Chief Joseph and his

Wallowa Lake and Wallowa Mountains
(Dept. of Interior, Nez Perce National Historical Park)

people had a deep love for the Valley of Winding Water, the burial ground of their ancestors.[1]

The next day Chief Joseph took a piece of parchment and drew a detailed map of the land they had been given in the treaty. This map was very accurate showing most of the geographic features of the area. When the map was finished, Chief Joseph called a small group of warriors together, including both Young Joseph and Ollikut. When they were assembled he said, "This paper shows the land that is now ours. We must guard the land carefully, as the white man sometimes forgets what he has promised. Tomorrow we will start riding around our land, placing markers to show what is ours. These markers will tell the white man that the land is ours and he is not to enter."

It took about ten days to ride around their land placing the markers. Today a few stone markers can be found, presumably some of the markers that were placed by Old Chief Joseph.[2]

The rest of the summer was spent collecting food for the coming winter. Smoke tents were erected with an interior framework to hold strips of venison and elk meat. Below the meat was a smoldering fire of alder wood. It took about a week for the meat to cure and dry and become the jerky they would eat during the winter. In addition to jerky, a group of women and young girls were assigned the task of berry picking. While this was usually considered a social activity, great care had to be taken. Bears were also very fond of berries and were particularly dangerous when the mother bears were out with their cubs.

Late in the summer Chief Joseph told his followers, "It is now time to meet our brothers on the Camas Prairie, to visit and to collect the camas root for our winter food."

It took several days to pack their possessions and prepare for the trip. Chief Joseph led his band over a well known trail that headed north by east crossing both the Snake and Salmon Rivers. These rivers were at their summertime low, so there was no difficulty in crossing. Upon leaving the Salmon River, they climbed up out of the Salmon River Canyon and emerged on the Camas Prairie. This prairie is a high plateau close to the newly formed village of Grangeville, Idaho.

Chief Joseph and his people were happy to see the camps of several other Nez Perce bands that had already arrived for the fall harvest of roots. Joseph placed his camp near those of White Bird, Looking Glass, and Lawyer, located close to Tolo Lake near the western edge of the Camas Prairie.

While the women were busy talking and gathering roots, the young warriors were out in the nearby hills hunting for game. Young Joseph and Ollikut now had their own rifles and were able to help in these hunts. These hunts would provide good training in marksmanship which they would find most useful in a few short years. Bullets were not plentiful because the trading posts were often reluctant to sell large quantities of ammunition to the Indians for fear of an uprising. Each morning Chief Joseph gave each of his sons two bullets. He then told them, "My sons, you must learn to hit your target on the first shot. Your game will not stand around waiting for you to shoot again. The next bullet gives you a chance at a second target, should you be lucky enough to find one." Neither Young Joseph nor Ollikut wanted to disappoint their father. Soon they became excellent marksmen.

Each evening was spent feasting, visiting and playing various tribal games. After a month, enough camas roots, a mainstay of the Nez Perce diet, had been collected and roasted to take care of some of their winter food needs. The roasting of the camas roots was accomplished by digging a pit and building a fire at the bottom of the pit. After a large bed of coals had been accumulated, it was covered with a layer of wet moss, followed by a layer of camas roots, and another layer of moss. This routine was continued until the pit was about three-quarters full. At this point another fire was built on top and allowed to burn until a bed of coals was formed. The pit was then filled with dirt and left for several days until the camas roots were roasted. When the camas roots were dug up, they could be described as a soft mess with a taste very much like licorice.

With this task completed, Chief Looking Glass and Chief Lawyer gathered their people and left for their winter homes in the valleys of the Clearwater River. Chief White Bird took his people back to the Salmon River country, while Chief Joseph took his people back to the Lapwai Mission where they had started the previous spring.

Chief Joseph kept his people around the Lapwai Mission for several years. He still felt that the white man's strength in battle came from his religion. During this time, they were faithful to their religious teachings but still retained many of their Indian customs.

However, it wasn't too long before unrest started to grow among the Nez Perce people. When gold was discovered in Idaho, miners started flocking onto the Indian reservation. The head chiefs of the Nez Perce gathered at Fort Lapwai and demanded that the government protect their land. A message was sent to the Bureau of Indian Affairs, and another council meeting was held in May of 1863. At this council, the commissioners proposed reducing the size of the Nez Perce reservation from about five thousand square miles to a little over five hundred square miles. The proposed reservation would include all of the land along the south side of the South Fork of the Clearwater River. All of the land in the Wallowa Valley and along the Salmon River would be lost to the Nez Perce.

Since the newly proposed reservation was primarily land already claimed by Chief Lawyer, he and some of the lesser nearby chiefs promptly signed the treaty. However, Chief Joseph, Chief White Bird, Chief Looking Glass, Chief Eagle-from-the-Light and another chief, Too hool hool zote, refused to sign the treaty which would take away their lands. The council, led to believe that Chief Lawyer was the head chief of all the Nez Perce people, demanded that all Nez Perce groups abide by the treaty. From that point on, the white leaders considered the Nez Perce as either "Treaty" or "Nontreaty" groups.

Old Chief Joseph was now convinced that he could not trust the words or teachings of the white man. Based on this new conviction, he tore up his copy of the treaty, along with his copy of the New Testament, and returned with his people to the Wallowa Valley. He stayed in the valley until his death in 1871.[3]

On his deathbed, he called Young Joseph and said, "My son, you are now the chief. Always remember that your father never sold this country. You must stop your ears whenever you are asked to sign a treaty selling your home. A few more years and white men will be all around you. They have their eyes on this land. My son, never forget my dying words. This country holds your father's body. Never sell the bones of your father and your mother." With these words Old Chief Joseph closed his eyes and left this world.[4]

Chapter 5

Young Chief Joseph

Joseph was only thirty-one years of age when he replaced his father as head chief of the Wallowa Nez Perce. From that point on he was no longer called Young Joseph, but was known throughout the Nez Perce nation as Chief Joseph. Chief Joseph was a born diplomat, not a warrior at heart. He would much rather reason his opponents into agreement than attain a position by fighting.

Shortly after the death of Old Chief Joseph, a delegation of white leaders traveled to Wallowa to try to persuade Chief Joseph to give up the land and return to the Lapwai reservation. Joseph explained his

Chief Joseph in native dress
Photo taken approximately 1899
(Montana Historical Society Research Center)

position in the following words: "If we ever owned the land we own it still, for I have never sold it. In the Treaty Council the commissioners claimed that our country had been sold to the government. Suppose a white man should come to me and say, 'Joseph, I like your horses and I want to buy them.' I say to him, 'No my horses suit me fine and I will not sell them.' Then he goes to my neighbor and says to him, 'Joseph has some good horses that I want to buy, but he refuses to sell.' My neighbor says, 'Pay me the money and I will sell you Joseph's horses.' The white man returns to me and says, 'Joseph I have bought your horses, and you must let me have them.' If we have ever sold our land to the government, that is the way it was bought."[1]

The white delegation returned to Fort Lapwai and reported to Indian Agent John B. Monteith that Chief Joseph had rejected their proposal. This brought about a flurry of letters and meetings concerning the Nez Perce position. Many prominent white leaders felt that the government should abide by the Treaty of 1855, and since the Wallowa Nez Perce had not signed the Treaty of 1863, they should not be held to it. The other side insisted that the white settlers had more rights to the land than the Indians; therefore, they should not be stopped from making their land claims.

The Wallowa Valley was considered unsuitable for farming. The land was too rugged and too difficult to reach from the outside. Also, the growing season was too short because of the elevation. However, ranchers considered the lower reaches of the valley excellent grazing land for their cattle.

Clashes between the ranchers and the Nez Perce soon broke out. Shortly after Joseph became chief, a group of ranchers, out looking for lost stock, came to the camp of two Nez Perce hunters and accused them of stealing their horses. One of the ranchers called out in a loud voice, "We have lost some horses, and we know you have stolen them."

The Nez Perce denied the charge. "We have not stolen your horses. Why would we steal your horses when we have the finest horses in the Northwest?" There were more heated words and a fight broke out. During the course of the fight, a rancher shot one of the Nez Perce hunters. A few days later, the ranchers found their lost horses on their own range.[2]

When Joseph heard about the incident, he sent for Ollikut, who was now a sub-chief. Chief Joseph said, "My brother, select a small group of tribal elders and go to Fort Lapwai. You will find Agent Monteith. Tell him what has happened and ask him for the same justice that a white man would receive had we killed one of the ranchers." When Ollikut and his group reached Lapwai, they were told that the matter would be investigated.

Agent Monteith tried to resolve the dispute but with little success. He sent a proposal to Washington that the lower meadows of the Wallowa Valley be opened for settlement, and that the upper part of the valley, including Lake Wallowa, be set aside as a Nez Perce hunting ground. The proposal was rejected by the Bureau of Indian Affairs in Washington. At this point Chief Joseph sent a request to Agent Monteith. In the request he said, "My people desire to live in peace on the land of our ancestors. I ask permission to go to Washington to present our case to the white leaders of your country." The request was denied and the unrest continued.[3]

With the increasing numbers of miners and settlers moving into the area, tension between these

Ollikut - Joseph's brother
(Dept. of Interior, Nez Perce National Historical Park)

groups and the Nez Perce steadily grew. In the fall of 1876, the Nez Perce Chiefs assembled at Fort Lapwai to voice their complaints and ask for assistance in resolving the many problems. By this time Washington had decided that further negotiations were useless and demanded that the Nez Perce obey the new rulings.

The meeting between the Nez Perce Chiefs and the white leaders started on a warm afternoon in a small room in the army barracks at Fort Lapwai. The Indian chiefs were seated on blankets on one side of the room. General Howard and the other white leaders were seated on chairs in front of the Nez Perce. The air was becoming thick with pipe and cigar smoke. The meeting was opened by General Howard, who stood and delivered this message: "The Great White Father in Washington has given me orders to see that the Treaty of 1863 is obeyed. In addition, the Presidential Order of 1873 gives me the authority to move all of you to the reservation here at Lapwai."

With these words Chief Too hool hool zote jumped to his feet and said, "The white man tells us nothing but lies. We signed the treaty you presented at the Walla Walla council. We have lived by that treaty. Now you tell us the treaty is no longer good and we must move from our land along the Salmon River and the Valley of Winding Waters and live on a small piece of ground here at Lapwai. I will not obey that order, and I will not sit here and listen to more of your lies." With these words, Chief Too hool hool zote turned his back on the white leaders and strode from the room.

As soon as Chief Too hool hool zote had left the building, Howard turned to an aid and instructed him to summon the guards, arrest the chief and place him in the stockade.[4]

Howard then continued with his orders from Washington. Each Nez Perce family was to be given twenty acres of land on the Lapwai reservation. The Nez Perce argued that this area was too small for their herds of horses and cattle. The meeting with the white leaders continued for several days.

Joseph and the other chiefs held many discussions on what they should do. Joseph decided it would be futile to oppose the whites. He reluctantly decided to agree with the new order. One condition the Nez Perce demanded was that Chief Too hool hool zote be released from the stockade.

In the early spring of 1877, Chief Joseph went to Agent Monteith and said, "Help from the white man is not coming. We can no longer oppose your orders. My people will move to our new home on the Lapwai reservation. We have been given one month to collect our livestock and other possessions. This is not enough time, and we request more time to do this." Agent Monteith would not agree to this request.

Chief Joseph took his people back to the Wallowa Valley and immediately started rounding up cattle and horses. Because the cattle had been on the range for so long they were now wild. The Nez Perce could collect only a small portion of their herd.

On the trip back to Lapwai, they had to take their livestock across both the Snake and Salmon Rivers which were now at flood stage. At the Snake River many of the cattle stampeded and were lost. Others were lost during the crossing. When they finally reached the Salmon River, they left some of the cattle behind and proceeded on to Tolo Lake to meet with the other Nez Perce groups who were gathered there. They planned to go together to Fort Lapwai on June 14th, the date set by General Howard.

A few days prior to that, Chief Joseph took his people back across the Salmon River. Their intent was to butcher some of their cattle and to allow the women time to gather and dry kause roots. Kause root was another staple of the Nez Perce diet. The root could be eaten either cooked or raw. For their winter food, the root was cooked, ground into a fine pulp and dried into small bricks. When the roots were prepared in this manner, the taste was very similar to stale biscuits. Because of this taste, the early settlers gave the plant the English name Biscuitroot.[5]

While Chief Joseph and his people were busy butchering cattle and gathering kause roots, the other Nez Perce groups remained at Tolo Lake waiting for the time to proceed to the Lapwai reservation.

The tribal elders devoted much of their time around the council fire discussing what to expect after their arrival at the Lapwai reservation. Many of the young warriors disagreed with what the chiefs and tribal elders were planning to do. Some of the more outspoken young men paraded through the campsite telling anyone who would listen what they would do if they were in charge. One of the more vocal of the braves was Wahlitits, a young warrior with Chief White

Bird's group. This continued until one of the tribal elders called to him and said, "Wahlitits, you have been telling everyone how brave you are. If you are so brave, why don't you kill the man who killed your father, Eagle Robe?"

The rebuke hurt Wahlitits' Indian pride. Early on the morning of June 13th, he called to his two cousins Sarpis Lipplip and Swan Necklace saying, "Follow me to the Salmon River country and let us kill the man who killed my father and your uncle." They were looking for Larry Ott who had murdered Eagle Robe. However, Larry Ott got word of their coming and, disguised as a Chinese miner, escaped into the mines along the Salmon River. When Wahlitits and his cousins couldn't find Larry Ott, they went to a nearby ranch whose owner was a known Indian-hater. The rancher was killed and the Nez Perce trio took his guns, ammunition and one of his horses.[6]

Shortly after Wahlitits and his cousins left Tolo Lake, a small group of about seventeen warriors left camp to join them. By early morning of June 14th, they joined forces and went on a killing spree up and down the Salmon River. They limited their targets to those white men who had either killed or harmed the

Nez Perce people. Over the next two days, approximately fifteen settlers were killed. By the afternoon of the 15th, word had begun to filter back about the many settlers who were being murdered. Settlers from surrounding communities were sending messages to Lapwai demanding military protection.

The tribal leaders, while camped around Tolo Lake, realized that war with the white man could no longer be avoided. Based on this premonition, the Nez Perce broke camp and retreated to the base of White Bird Canyon, a distance of about 7 miles, where they set up a temporary camp and waited for the arrival of the military forces.

Chief Joseph was on his way back up to Tolo Lake when he met the retreating Nez Perce groups. This was the first knowledge he had had of the killings along the Salmon River Valley. Even though he had tried for many years to avoid any conflict, he knew that a peaceful settlement could no longer be attained.

When the messengers from the settlement arrived at Fort Lapwai asking for military protection, General O. O. Howard agreed that something had to be done.

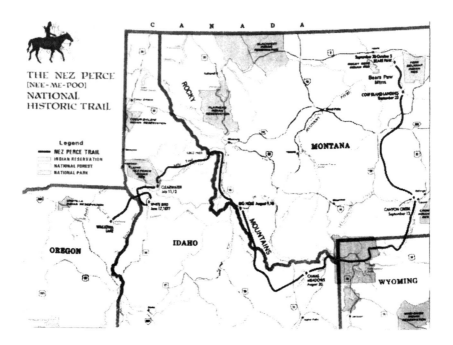

(Forest Service, U.S. Department of Agriculture)

Chapter 6

Start of the Nez Perce War

On June 14, 1877, General Howard arrived at Fort Lapwai to await the arrival of the Nez Perce. The following day, after receiving reports from the white settlers of the murders being committed, Howard decided that a peaceful relocation of the Nez Perce to the Lapwai reservation was impossible. By that evening, he had assembled two companies of cavalry under the command of Captain Perry. Perry was given orders to proceed immediately to White Bird Canyon and bring Joseph and the other Nez Perce groups to Lapwai, using force if necessary.

When Perry and his ninety-nine troopers were ready to leave the fort, General Howard said, "God speed, Captain. You must not let the Indians beat you." Perry replied with a smile, "General, I have very little fear of that happening."[1]

By the following evening, Perry and his troops had reached Grangeville, a distance of some seventy miles. They were exhausted and wanted to rest until the next morning, but the settlers were too intent upon action. Heeding their demands, Perry gathered twelve volunteers from the settlers and proceeded to the upper rim of White Bird Canyon. There they rested until the morning of June 17.

Late in the evening of June 16, two young Nez Perce horse herders reported seeing army troops heading toward the village of Grangeville. The Nez Perce held a war council led by Chief White Bird, Yellow Wolf and Ollikut. Their objective was to make plans for the defense of their people. Shortly after midnight, a soldier on guard duty struck a match to light his pipe. Immediately, the chilling sound of a coyote howling echoed through the canyon. A Nez Perce scout had just sent a warning of the army's presence.

General Oliver O. Howard
(Dept. of Interior, Nez Perce National Historical Park)

Early on the morning of June 17, Perry started his troops down a draw to the base of White Bird Canyon some 3,000 feet below. About halfway down, the troops were surprised to see a small band of Nez Perce approaching carrying a white flag. Chief Joseph was making a final attempt at a peaceful settlement with the army. Unfortunately, two of the cavalry fired at the peace envoy. Though both shots missed, the Nez Perce responded with a volley of shots. Perry's bugler was killed, and was the first casualty of the White Bird battle. When he realized the bugler was dead, Perry ordered the troopers to charge down the canyon.[2]

During the night, a group of Nez Perce warriors had proceeded a short distance up White Bird Creek and were spread out along the base of the hill, well hidden behind rocks and brush. Thus, the charge of the mounted troops allowed the Nez Perce to have warriors on both sides and to the front of the troops. The mounted soldiers were further surprised when a herd of horses were stampeded through their ranks. Unknown to the soldiers, there were warriors clinging to the sides of many of the horses. Perry's forces were now completely surrounded.

In a short time, the canyon was filled with dust and a white cloud of gun smoke. The Nez Perce soon proved their superior marksmanship as dead and wounded soldiers covered the hillside. Most of the remaining cavalry forgot about fighting the Indians. Their only concern was saving their own lives. As they started retreating back up White Bird Hill, all semblance of military discipline was lost. This made it much easier for the Nez Perce to race after and kill the fleeing soldiers. The retreating army made very little effort to save or rescue their wounded companions, who lay screaming for help on the ground. The Nez Perce warriors pursued the army back to Grangeville.[3]

When the battle of White Bird was over, Perry had lost thirty-four of his ninety-nine cavalrymen, with two more wounded. The Nez Perce had two warriors wounded and none killed. Following the armies' retreat from the battleground, Chief Joseph called all of the Nez Perce together and said, "We will show the white man that we do not fight like savages. We will not scalp or mutilate any dead soldier. We will take only articles of war that will be of use to us." With these words, the warriors returned to the battlefield and collected all of the guns and ammunition they could find.[4]

That evening a celebration was held honoring the warriors who had defended the Nez Perce encampment. Ollikut, the leader of the young warriors, arose during the celebration and said, "My people, today you have witnessed many acts of bravery by our warriors. They have shown their bravery and cunning in the face of superior odds. We can feel safe when these young men fight as they did today."

Chief Joseph, not as elated over the victory as Ollikut was, kept his distance from the celebration. Later that evening during a council of the chiefs and tribal elders, he arose and said, "My brothers, today our warriors won a great victory. It is my fear that this victory will be short-lived. The army can call in many more soldiers than we have people in the entire Nez Perce nation. Our only hope is to leave our homeland and travel to the land of the Sioux or the Crow." After some thought he continued, "We must find time to gather our people and supplies for the long trip to the Montana Territory. Tomorrow we will go back across the Salmon River to make plans for our departure.

The white man's army will find it too difficult to cross the river to pursue us."

The next morning while the women were packing their family possessions, another council of chiefs and tribal elders was held. During this council, Chief Looking Glass rose and said, "My brothers, we are entering a difficult time for our people. I do not wish to be in a war that I know we can not win. This morning I will take my people and we will return to our home on the Clearwater River. We will live there in peace. Our hopes will ride with you as we may never see each other again." With these words, Chief Looking Glass took his people and started for the Clearwater River.

Two days later Perry returned to Fort Lapwai and reported to Howard. The general was amazed at the accuracy of the Indian rifle fire and their apparent knowledge of military tactics. It never occurred to Howard that it was not so much superior military tactics by the Indians as it was errors made by his own troopers during the battle.

General Howard immediately sent messages to nearby military commands requesting reinforcements. A large contingent of soldiers soon arrived from Fort

Walla Walla along with a group of volunteers. On June 24, an army of over 400 men started for White Bird Canyon under the leadership of General Howard. On June 27 they arrived at the scene of the White Bird battle and found the slain soldiers lying where they had fallen. They were buried as rapidly as possible at the spot where they had fallen. That night, General Howard set up camp on the banks of the Salmon River.[5]

The next morning when the troops arose, the Nez Perce on the far side of the river were yelling and taunting them to come over and fight. Later that day, General Howard ordered his troops to cross the river.

Meanwhile, the Nez Perce had ridden about twenty-five miles down river and gone back across the Salmon River. While the army was temporarily stuck on the far side of the Salmon River, the Nez Perce retreated across the Camas Prairie and on toward the Clearwater River.[6]

The young braves did not show the concern and worry felt by Chief Joseph. The day was clear and sunny and they had beaten and outsmarted the army twice. With these victories, they did not understand Chief Joseph's sense of urgency. Instead, they were in high spirits, laughing and joking about the army's problems in crossing the river. They gloated over their ability to outsmart the army, by tricking them into crossing the river.

As soon as possible, General Howard sent a message to Captain Whipple, who had been left to protect Grangeville, to assemble his men and go in pursuit of the fleeing Nez Perce. Whipple was also ordered to bring Chief Looking Glass back to Grangeville for safe keeping.

Chapter 7

Escape to the Clearwater

Captain Whipple, in command of two companies of troops, proceeded at once to the middle fork of the Clearwater River. He knew this to be the ancestral home of Chief Looking Glass. Whipple arrived at the Indian village at dawn on July 1. One of Whipple's scouts, a man who had married a Nez Perce woman, was fluent in their language. The scout was sent to summon the chief. From a nearby hill he called out, "Chief Looking Glass, our Captain wants to talk to you." Chief Looking Glass did not trust the army so he sent one of his elders, Peo Pco Tholekt, to see

Peo Peo Tah Likt
(Dept. of Interior, Nez Perce National Historical Park)

what the Captain wanted. This did not satisfy Whipple. He again had his scout call out that he wanted to talk to Chief Looking Glass.

When the second demand came, Chief Looking Glass became very suspicious. He sent Peo Peo Tholekt and another tribal elder back to Whipple to deliver a message that he had no fight with the white man. "We want to live in peace. Go away and leave us alone." As the message was being delivered shots rang out, and Peo Peo Tholekt was wounded in the leg. The other tribal elder was killed. Chief Looking Glass and the rest of the village immediately mounted horses and escaped into the woods.[1]

Chief Looking Glass and his people rode about two miles up river to a small meadow. They soon could see and smell smoke coming from their village. Chief Looking Glass sent a couple of scouts back to determine what was happening and what the army was going to do next. They soon reported that Whipple had burned down all of the tepees and had laid waste to their gardens. They also reported that Whipple and his troops were heading back in the direction of the Camas Prairie. When Chief Looking Glass learned what had happened, he immediately decided to find and rejoin with Chief Joseph and the other Nez Perce groups on their journey to the Montana Territory.

Following the raid on Chief Looking Glass and his village, Whipple and his troops returned to the Camas Prairie. Whipple sent two scouts to see if any Indians remained in the area. The scouts soon encountered the rear guard of the main Nez Perce force. When the Indians saw them, they immediately gave chase with loud war whoops and the thunder of horses' hooves. During the chase, one of the scouts was killed but the other got away.

When the scout reported back to Whipple, he did not know that his companion had been killed. Captain Whipple sent out Lieutenant Rains and ten select troops to determine the Nez Perce strength and to rescue the fallen scout if he was still alive. The troopers were spotted by Five Wounds, one of the Nez Perce scouts, and a small group of warriors who immediately gave chase. The Indians were finding that war with the army was exhilarating if not downright fun. During the initial chase, two of the soldiers were killed. The remaining cavalry tried to escape with the Indians in full pursuit. The army horses were soon winded, and the troopers took cover behind any rock or bush they could find. Before long Lieutenant Rains and all of his men were killed. Even though the army fired many rounds of ammunition, not one Indian or horse was hit.[2] When Ollikut heard of this skirmish, he said to Five Wounds, "Does this not again prove that the Nez Perce are much better shots than the army troops?"

By this time the settlers were becoming quite disgusted with the army. Their general feeling was best described when one of the settlers told the army, "We will receive more protection from the leniency of Chief Joseph than we will ever receive from you people."

General Howard and his troops finally arrived on the Camas Prairie. When briefed by Whipple, particularly on the Chief Looking Glass raid, General Howard commented, "All we have done is stir up a hornet's nest. Joseph now has many more warriors to help with his fighting."

Colonel McConville was stationed at Mount Idaho to protect that community. The settlers were very upset with how easily the army was being defeated by the Nez Perce. At their urging, McConville assembled a group of about eighty volunteers and took off after the Nez Perce. When he approached where he thought the Nez Perce might be, he felt it wise to travel on higher ground. However, on Doty Ridge, just east of the Clearwater River, his company was fired upon by Indian sharpshooters.

McConville had his men dig in, with orders that no fires were to be lit during the night. Ollikut and his braves kept up sporadic gunfire most of the night. Two horses were killed, but the Indians captured a herd of about forty-eight army horses. No soldiers or Indians were killed.

The army volunteers spent the night with no heat and very little food or water. The next morning, with no sign of Indians in the area, McConville and his men made a hasty retreat back to Mount Idaho. Because of the conditions the army endured that night, Doty Ridge was renamed "Misery Hill."[3]

Chief Joseph soon heard about Chief Looking Glass and the destruction of his village. Knowing that Chief Looking Glass had no place to go, Joseph expected him to join his group. A few days later the two chiefs did meet just above the junction of the South and Middle Forks of the Clearwater River. Chief

Looking Glass spoke first. "My people were living in peace. We had no desire to do battle with the white man. The white man did not honor our intentions. They brought the war to us, wounding and killing some of my people, taking many of our horses and destroying our homes. We have no choice but to join you in this battle of survival."

Chief Joseph answered in the following manner, "My brother, you are welcome. Our people need your help and guidance. Because of your many years of hunting buffalo, you know the trails into the Montana Territory. You also have many friends among the Sioux and the Crow where we must go to live. We do not seek war. We have left our homes, trying to avoid General Howard and his troops. When we get to the Montana Territory our journey should be over and we can live in peace."

The combined groups of Nez Perce made camp at the junction of the two rivers. Chief Joseph knew his people needed rest before starting the difficult journey over the Lolo Trail. The chiefs that were present also wanted time to discuss plans for the future. There were now five different Nez Perce bands grouped together. Decisions had to be made on the leadership of the massed group. It was soon decided that Chief White Bird and Chief Too hool hool zote would act as war chiefs, and Chief Joseph would be responsible for the well being of the people.

During the second day of these discussions, a scouting party under the direction of Ollikut rode into camp and announced that soldiers were approaching from the east. Howard had arrived with a massed army of 400 men and over 100 volunteers. When Howard topped a ridge, he saw the Nez Perce camp below him. Howard's first action was to spread out his men and approach the Nez Perce encampment. The Indian warriors made a similar movement, starting uphill to meet the army, trying to outflank the soldiers. As they approached the troops, they reverted to typical Indian tactics, darting from tree to tree or to any protective cover they could find. As soon as the Indians came within range of the troops, both sides started shooting. In a short time the air was filled with dust and the white haze of gun smoke. The sound of rifle and cannon fire echoed through the river valley, along with the screams and yells of wounded soldiers and Indians. Above all of this noise was the eerie keening of the women when they saw one of their family members hit during the heat of battle.

The major difference between the Indians and the army was that the army was under the command of one person, General Howard, while the Indians fought as separate units under their own chief. To quite an extent, the Indians also fought as separate individuals. Because of this, the army was much better organized. In addition, General Howard had managed to bring a howitzer. After digging in the wheels so they could lower the barrel, they were able to fire directly into the Indian encampment.

Red Fox, a young warrior, was about to dash to another tree when he glanced down the hill at the Indian encampment. Just at that moment a cannon ball hit one of the tepees, completely destroying it. Red Fox was stunned, for the tepee was the home of one of his close friends. With a wild yell he completely forgot about his own safety and raced into the middle of the army line. He started shooting at anything he saw move, and when his rifle was empty, he used it as a club. Red Fox killed three soldiers before he himself was mortally wounded.

Chief Joseph, fighting the soldiers halfway up the hill, saw the destruction the cannon was making. He realized the extreme danger the women and children were facing. Chief Joseph returned to the camp and directed the women, old men, and children to pack what was absolutely necessary, cross the river and head for the Weippe meadows on the way to the Lolo Trail. The war chiefs left a small group of warriors behind to keep the army pinned down, allowing time for the Nez Perce to escape.[4]

When General Howard reached the river where the Nez Perce had crossed, he found the water too deep and fast for the army. However, a few miles down river at Greer, the miners had built a ferry across the Clearwater River. Howard proceeded down river to the ferry. Before Howard reached the site, an army scout raced back and finding the general said, "General, them durn Injuns have cut that ferry loose and it is now grounded on the far side of the river."

When General Howard was finally able to cross the Clearwater River, he headed for the small community of Kamiah, where he made camp for about ten days. Although General Howard was receiving much criticism from his superiors for his inability to beat the Nez Perce, he felt that the battle of the Clearwater was a clear indication that he was making progress He spent ten days in Kamiah writing letters and sending messages to the army headquarters in San Francisco and Washington, D.C. In general, these messages said, "We have stopped the Nez Perce and they are no longer a threat to the settlers of the Idaho Territory." In a dispatch to San Francisco, he further said, "We still have to capture the Nez Perce, but that should not take too long."

The Nez Perce held a different view of the situation. Yellow Wolf, who fought in the battle at the Clearwater and later became a Nez Perce historian, made the following assessment, "We have not been beaten. Had we been beaten, we could not have escaped from the Clearwater with our lives."

The Nez Perce had developed a unique system of signals to keep their people informed where the army was located and what they were doing. It soon became apparent that the army was very slow in its pursuit of the Nez Perce. Because of these delays, Chief Too hool hool zote gave Howard the nickname "General Day After Tomorrow." The Nez Perce felt quite secure in their ability to stay ahead of the army.[5]

Ollikut and his young warriors kept close track of the army camp. As long as the army stayed in one place, the Nez Perce would also stay in their camp. The women used this time to replace some of the equipment they had lost when they left the Clearwater camp. These were items such as travois and tepee poles and deerskin bags to hold berries and roots. In addition, they had time to dry and smoke meat which would be used on their travels to Montana.

A council of the Nez Perce chiefs was held at Weippe. In this council, definite long-range plans were made. It was decided to go on the Lolo Trail into the Montana Territory, then south and east to the land of the Crow. Chief Looking Glass was primarily responsible for the route they would take to the Crow People and to his many friends in that tribe.

Chapter 8

Trail to Montana

At the Weippe Meadow camp site, the Nez Perce held their final council. Chief Looking Glass and Chief Too hool hool zote, along with several principal warriors, spoke long and believably on why they should travel to the land of the Crow. On the other hand, Chief Joseph was not entirely convinced when he said, "Why are we fighting this war if not to save the land of our ancestors? I will take my people to the land of the Crow. When things are again calm, I will return with my people to the land that we all love."

The following morning Chief Looking Glass led the Nez Perce east. Upon reaching the start of the

Lolo trail, the war chiefs told Ollikut to select some of his best warriors to bring up the rear. This was to ensure that they were not overtaken by any army units. Chief Looking Glass was not too concerned about the army following them over the Lolo trail. The trail was too rugged and narrow to allow the passage of any supply wagons, and, above all, the howitzer General Howard had brought to the Clearwater.[1]

Establishing a rear guard was a strategic move by the Nez Perce. As soon as Howard heard that the Nez Perce were on the move, he sent Colonel McConville with a strong force of cavalry and Indian scouts in hot pursuit. The pursuit did not last very long for the Indian scouts of the army were soon ambushed. This sent McConville and his cavalry back to Kamiah. However, three of Ollikuts warriors had been hit. One was killed instantly and another died later. Several of Ollikuts warriors followed McConville back to Kamiah where they recaptured several hundred head of horses that had been taken from the Nez Perce. These horses were taken back up the Lolo trail to the main body of the Nez Perce.[2]

The Lolo Trail crossing the Bitterroot Mountains, between Idaho and Montana, is the same trail over which Sacajawea had led Lewis and Clark during their voyage to the Pacific Ocean. In general, the trail follows the Lochsa River from where it enters the Clearwater River to its origin near Lolo Pass. The Lolo Trail, about 150 miles long, had been used for centuries by Indian hunters traveling between Idaho and Montana. No improvements had ever been made to the trail. In fact, Indians sometimes became lost trying to follow it. The general course of the trail is very steep, narrow and rocky, along mountain ridges separated from each other by deep ravines. In many places it passes through dense forests of pine, fir, spruce and cedar, with a dense undergrowth of brush.[3]

At the start of the trip into Montana, Chief Joseph summoned all of the Nez Perce together and made the following statement; "We are leaving our home in Idaho and traveling to an unknown future in Montana. We will do no harm to any white man in Montana. Our war is with the army in Idaho. In Montana we hope to find peace and safety."

Howard stayed in Kamiah developing his war plans. Knowing it would be impossible to take wagons and his howitzer over the Lolo Trail, he divided his force into what he called right and left columns. One column under Colonel Wheaton would travel north into Montana by way of the Mullan road then proceed to Missoula.

Howard took the other column of cavalry and infantry over the Lolo Trail. Before leaving Kamiah, Howard sent a wire to Fort Missoula stating that the Nez Perce were coming and that the Missoula personnel should detain them until he could arrive.

The Indians had many advantages over the army. The women could pitch a tent, take it down and pack it on a horse with more precision than the army ever could. The Nez Perce also had distinct divisions of labor; there were hunters, horse herders, and berry and root pickers. Each person knew his job and did it efficiently. In addition, the Indians knew the roots and plants that could be used for food when game and fish were scarce. The pursuing army was mystified as to why so many trees were scarred. They did not know that the inner bark provided good nourishment.

Because of their efficiency, Chief Joseph and the Nez Perce reached the 7,000-foot summit of the Lolo Trail in about eleven days. On the eleventh day they reached Lolo Creek, an easy day's ride from where it enters the Bitterroot River. There were many hot springs in the area. The place which the Nez Perce called Salmon Creek had been earlier named by Lewis and Clark as "Travelers Rest." Here Chief Joseph and the other chiefs decided to rest and hold council.

The Lolo Trail passes through a narrow gap into the Bitterroot Valley. Nez Perce scouts soon discovered the army had built a log breastwork or barricade across this narrow portion of the trail. The Nez Perce did not know Howard had sent a wire to Missoula requesting that the army detain the Nez Perce until he could arrive. Captain Rawn from Fort Missoula had been sent with a detail of thirty men to detain the Nez Perce. His detail had built the log barricade across the canyon.

The discovery of the log barricade did not seem to worry the Nez Perce. A hasty council was called to decide upon an alternate route to the Bitterroot Valley. The following morning Chief Looking Glass led the Nez Perce along a mountain ridge above the log barricade. The first knowledge Rawn had of the Nez Perce presence was when one of his privates called out, "Captain, look up the ridge to the north. There go all of the Injuns we were supposed to stop." The Nez Perce were out of rifle range, but Rawn and his men could now hear them laughing and singing as they passed. It wasn't too long before the log barricade was given the name "Fort Fizzle."[4]

The Bitterroot Valley is a long narrow valley, bordered on the west by the snow capped peaks of the Bitterroot Range and on the east by the Continental Divide. The Bitterroot River runs down the middle of the valley. The Bitterroot Valley, a pristine area, was the hunting ground of the Salish Indians, who were on very friendly terms with the Nez Perce. Although this was Indian land, some farms, ranches and small towns were beginning to appear.

The days were warm and sunny, and the air was crisp and clear, so Chief Looking Glass set a very leisurely pace through the valley. The Chiefs felt their war was now over and they could start living in peace. The only dissenting vote came from Chief White Bird, who did not feel that the Nez Perce should join with the Crow people. He was in favor of a rapid retreat to Canada to join forces with the Sioux who had escaped from the army after the battle of Little Big Horn.

About three days into the Bitterroot Valley, the Nez Perce came to a ranch which they carefully went around. However, a small group of warriors from

Chief Too hool hool zote's band found the ranch house vacant and stole a supply of food and clothing. When Chief Looking Glass heard what had happened, he immediately called the warriors together and said, "We have entered Montana as a peaceful people. To keep the peace and to show our intentions, we will not harm any of the people or take any of their belongings without first paying for what we take. To pay for what you have taken, you will select seven of your finest horses, put the rancher's brand on those horses, and leave them in the ranch corral."[5]

The Nez Perce now had a problem. There were many trails they could take on leaving the Bitterroot Valley. The trail Chief White Bird preferred led across the Blackfoot River and northeast into Canada. The other chiefs were more interested in hunting buffalo, hoping they could live in peace. While there were many routes to the buffalo grounds, most had the disadvantage of passing close to large towns and army posts where the army could intercept them. The route finally chosen was much longer, but did not have the problems of the other trails. This trail led south to the Big Hole Basin, then swung east to the Crow and buffalo country.

The chiefs kept the Nez Perce at a steady but leisurely pace on their way to the Big Hole Basin. Eight days passed from the time they outsmarted Rawn until their arrival at the Big Hole Basin. The Nez Perce set up camp along the Big Hole River for an extended rest.

The Big Hole is a vast open basin at the foot of the Continental Divide in the Beaverhead Mountains, bordered on the west by a high mountain range and on the east by low foothills sloping up to a tableland. Chief Looking Glass chose a campsite on a large grassy meadow with the Big Hole River winding through it. Along the upper edge of the meadow were thick groves of lodgepole pine where the women could cut tepee poles to replace those lost at the Clearwater battlefield. The council decided to set up a semi-permanent camp to give everyone a chance to rest and relax after the long journey.

Several warriors, including Wahlitits, told anyone who would listen about their dreams of death and destruction which would be coming very soon. However, the council of war chiefs felt their war was over and further precautions were unnecessary. In addition, Chief Looking Glass felt the white settlers would consider it a hostile act if scouts were sent out. Because of this, no rear guard was established nor were scouts sent out to determine if any troops were in the area.[6]

Chapter 9

Battle at the Big Hole Basin

Before leaving Kamiah, General Howard had sent a wire to Fort Missoula asking that they hold the Nez Perce until he could arrive.

On July 30, three days after the Nez Perce had passed "Fort Fizzle," Howard left Kamiah in a pouring rain storm and started over the Lolo Trail. Howard's column of cavalry, infantry and pack mules made a caravan about two miles long. All of the pack mules were necessary to carry food and other supplies for the soldiers. Unlike the Indians, the soldiers didn't know how to live off the land. In addition, the army horses were not as used to the rugged mountain terrain as were the Indian horses. Because of heavy rain, many horses slipped on the rocks and fell into deep canyons. Also, the mules were reluctant to travel on the trail in the wet and slippery conditions. Much cussing, yelling and use of whips were necessary to keep the caravan moving.[1]

Soon after starting, they found that the Lolo Trail would have to be widened in many places in order for the pack mules to get through. This work was efficiently accomplished by a group of Idaho frontiersmen who had volunteered to accompany Howard. The cavalry soon found it necessary to take very good care of their horses. If a horse were to become lame or for some other reason could not proceed, the rider was assigned a place in the infantry as a foot soldier.

While Howard was starting over the Lolo Trail, Colonel Wheaton took the other column and headed north to cross into Montana by way of the Mullan Road. This was a sensible move since Wheaton could use wagons to carry supplies and could also transport the howitzer into Montana. Howard was hoping the two columns could reach Missoula at about the same time. Wheaten could then block the Nez Perce from heading north into Canada.

At the same time Howard's and Wheaton's columns were heading toward Montana, Colonel Gibbon was leaving Fort Shaw on the Sun River with about 150 troopers. Gibbon was heading for the Bitterroot Valley to try to intercept the Nez Perce. He also felt there was a possibility he might intercept the Nez Perce along the Blackfoot River on one of the shorter trails to the buffalo country.

Gibbon was the first to arrive at Fort Missoula. Here he learned that the Nez Perce had traveled down the Bitterroot Valley and were heading for the Big Hole Basin. Howard had sent a messenger to find Gibbon. The message was for the Colonel not to take any military action until Howard could join forces with him. The messenger couldn't find Gibbon so it was never delivered. Gibbon, with no instructions from Howard, decided to start at once in pursuit of the Nez Perce. In addition, he had received no orders about prisoners or acts of leniency. Therefore, his only goal was complete destruction of the Nez Perce. With this goal in mind, he ordered a forced march toward the Big Hole Basin.[2]

While Gibbon was passing through the Bitterroot Valley, he was able to pick up some civilian volunteers. They told the Colonel they were joining for patriotic reasons, when in fact their primary goal was to steal Nez Perce horses.

Meanwhile, several Indian warriors offered to scout the Nez Perce back trail to see if any army units were following. In order to do this, they requested the loan of some fast horses. Chief Looking Glass rejected the offer, stating that this would be interpreted by the white man as an act of war. He also felt it would be against the policy of peace the Nez Perce wanted to present. Yellow Wolf, a Nez Perce warrior, had a different version of why the offer was rejected. He said, "Chief Looking Glass will reject any suggestion that he did not think of first."

Gibbon reached Ross Hole, about one day's march behind the Nez Perce. Upon their arrival, Lieutenant Bradley offered to take a company of cavalry and make a forced march to the Big Hole Basin. His objective was not to engage in battle but to scout the Indian encampment, determine their strength and develop battle plans. He also hoped to run off and capture any Indian horses if this could be done safely.[3]

Gibbon accepted the offer. Bradley and about sixty cavalry members started out that evening. By the following morning they had reached the outer rim of the Big Hole Basin. Bradley hid his men in a secluded valley away from the trail. After breakfast, he and a couple of scouts worked their way forward until they had a clear view of the Indian camp. From this vantage point they made an assessment of the Indian's strength and drew a detailed map of the Indian camp and the surrounding terrain.

The Indian encampment had the appearance of a peaceful settlement. A group of Indian women were seen in the foothills cutting and trimming lodgepole pine for tepee pole and travois supports. The children were swimming and playing along the banks of the Big Hole River. The tribal elders were seated around a small campfire talking and enjoying the warm sun beating down on their shoulders.

Of particular interest to Bradley was the arrangement of the tepees and closest available cover to them. Also of interest was a herd of about 300 horses grazing peacefully in a meadow across the river from the camp. When Lieutenant Bradley was satisfied that he had all the information needed, he and his two scouts quietly withdrew and returned to the valley where the rest of the troops were secluded. Leaving his sergeant in charge, Bradley returned to Gibbon to present his findings.

Gibbon immediately ordered his troops forward. By that evening he reached Bradley's force which was approximately six miles from the Indian village. Here he ordered a rest until eleven o'clock that night. At that time he wanted to draw closer and be in position to strike at the first sign of daylight.

At eleven o'clock the troops were awakened. Gibbon, with a force of approximately 130 men, started their cautious approach toward the Nez Perce village. All horses were left behind. The approach was made on foot in order to be as quiet as possible. By four in the morning, the soldiers had reached the rim of the Big Hole Basin about one mile from the Nez Perce camp. Here they took a small trail leading to a point directly west of the camp and that had good ground cover where the soldiers could hide. On the way to the area, they had to pass a herd of horses grazing on the hillside. The troops were quiet enough that the horses were not aroused, nor did any of the camp dogs pick up their scent and start barking. The troops were surprised that no herders were out guarding the horses.

Gibbon had been told by one of his scouts that if the Nez Perce were not aware of any danger, the women would come out about an hour before daybreak and start their cooking fires. As predicted, about an hour before sunup the women came out, replenished their fires, chatted for a few minutes and then returned to their tepees.

Each soldier knew his battle plan and the area of the camp he was to attack. The signal for attack was to be the first shot fired the instant their presence was discovered. All of the soldiers had been given strict orders that their initial volley of fire was to be almost at ground level into the tepees in order to kill as many of the sleeping Indians as they could. Shortly after the women had started their cooking fires, a lone warrior emerged from his tepee, mounted a horse and rode directly into the waiting soldiers. An immediate volley of fire killed the warrior and his horse, and the battle of the Big Hole Basin had begun.[4]

At the sound of rifle fire, the soldiers charged across the river and immediately started firing their rifles into the base of the tepees. Men, women and children were all equal targets.

The dazed Nez Perce came running out of their tepees trying to determine what was happening. In an effort to hide in the willow thickets along the river bank, most of the Nez Perce were running directly at the soldiers. Some of the Nez Perce had grabbed their rifles, but many had left them in their tepees. In a short time the chiefs were calling to the warriors to fight for their families and take revenge for the family and friends who had been killed.[5]

The wives of both Chief Joseph and Ollikut were wounded at the start of the battle. Chief Joseph picked up his baby daughter with one hand, his rifle with the other, and dashed to the river bank. There he found a woman hidden in the brush who took his daughter for safe keeping. He and Ollikut returned to the battle and fought with desperate fury.

The soldiers had orders to burn the Nez Perce village, but the tepees were too wet to ignite readily. Their attempts to get the fires started caused a lull in the battle. This lull gave many of the warriors the opportunity they needed to return to the tepees and collect the rifles they had left behind. It wasn't too long before the basin was shrouded with a layer of gun smoke. The cries and screams of the wounded women and children acted as a catalyst for the Nez Perce warriors to increase their efforts to repel the cowardly attack of the army on their village. Mingled among all of the noise was the loud distressing neighing of horses that had been hit by rifle fire. Passing through the army ranks was a horse dragging its left rear leg. The dazed look in the animal's eyes made it apparent that he was no longer aware of any battle going on around him.

As in previous engagements, the accuracy of the Nez Perce rifle fire was much better than that of the army. Warriors darted from cover to cover until they were well within range, then proceeded to fire upon the soldiers. Some warriors had mounted their horses and were riding back and forth in the hills behind the soldiers. From this vantage point they were able to shoot down at the barricaded troops. Most of the troops had retreated up a mountain side and had dug protective trenches behind fallen logs. This didn't seem to bother the Nez Perce. In one instance, a warrior had climbed a tree and shot four soldiers barricaded in one trench. At this point the warrior was spotted and he too was killed.

During the course of the battle, a group of warriors captured a pack mule carrying a large quantity of ammunition for Springfield rifles. Since many of those rifles had been captured during the battle, the extra supply of ammunition was a welcome prize.

About midmorning, the army brought up the howitzer. As soon as it was fired, a small band of warriors charged the gun emplacement, killing most of the crew. Since the warriors didn't know how to fire the howitzer, they dismantled it, rolled it down the hill, and buried it.[6]

About the time the howitzer was captured, Chief Joseph came to the realization that his primary responsibility was the care and welfare of the women, children and old men. He knew he would have to move these people out of harm's way. His initial task was to assemble a group of older men to gather up as many of the slain Indian bodies as they could find. These bodies were wrapped in robes and placed under cut-banks along the rivers edge. When this task was finished, Chief Joseph gathered his people and started the retreat, heading south back into Idaho Territory.

Chief Joseph was responsible for a very sad procession. Many travois had been rigged and wounded strapped to them. Children were screaming in pain from their bullet wounds and the jolting they received as their travois was dragged over the ground. As they were leaving, many of the warriors voiced their discontent with the leadership of Chief Looking Glass. They felt their losses were due to Chief Looking Glass' failure to heed the warnings of his people. He had not allowed them to travel through the country fast enough, nor had he allowed warriors to scout their back trail for approaching army troops. Because of this discontent, Chief Looking Glass was demoted, and Lean Elk became the war leader.[7]

While the Nez Perce escape was in progress, Ollikut was left in charge of about thirty warriors responsible for keeping the army pinned down. This they did until the following morning. At that time Ollikut called the warriors together and said, "If we kill one soldier, they have a hundred who will take his place. If we lose one warrior, there is no one to take his place. Let us leave."

Chapter 10

Escape to Yellowstone Park

Two days after the battle at the Big Hole Basin, General Howard and his replacements finally arrived. His arrival was welcomed because of the two doctors and the medical supplies that he brought with him. Colonel Gibbon's camp looked more like a hospital ward than an army camp.

When Gibbon saw Howard he immediately exclaimed, "General, you are a most welcome sight. We have no doctor and very few medical supplies. As you can see, we have many wounded who need fast medical treatment to keep them alive."

Howard replied in a very reserved manner, "Colonel, I have two doctors and all the medical supplies you will need, but first, why didn't you follow my orders? Had you followed those orders, this would never have happened."

"General, I never received any orders from you. My only instructions from Missoula were to overtake the Nez Perce, kill as many as possible and capture the rest. We would have accomplished that goal, but I have never seen a band of Indians that could fight harder and longer than the Nez Perce."[1]

At this point, Howard tried to get an assessment of the battle. It soon became apparent that no clear-cut victory could be given to either side. The army was amazed at the ferocity of the Nez Perce warriors. The evaluation of the battle placed it as one of the bloodiest and hardest fought battles of any Indian campaign.

Howard picked up about fifty volunteers from Gibbon's command, and on August 13, two days after his arrival at the Big Hole Basin, he started south in pursuit of Chief Joseph and the Nez Perce.

Chief Joseph headed south toward the Idaho Territory. The first afternoon they traveled about thirteen miles to a small creek and made camp. Although his people were cold and hungry, they spent their time taking care of the wounded, trying to make them as comfortable as possible. Chief Joseph seemed tireless, going around the encampment seeing to the care of the wounded, particularly the children. He also made sure that each wounded person had a blanket or robe for the night. He gave up his own robe to a young girl shot in the leg.

Lean Elk set up a rear guard with some of his warriors, who immediately built stone rifle pits. Some of these stone rifle pits are still evident today. Early the next morning, when the main body of Nez Perce were ready to travel, they were joined by the warriors guarding the rear.

Another defensive move by Lean Elk was to separate the family unit. The women, children and old men were sent ahead with the horse herders. The able-bodied warriors brought up the rear. Ranchers and hunters who by chance observed this body of warriors reported their sightings back to the nearest settlement. The settlements considered these warriors a potential warlike threat. They did not realize that they were there strictly for defensive purposes.

Chief Joseph had to travel more slowly because of all the wounded. The best they could do was about fifteen miles per day. It was not uncommon for soldiers who were following to come upon wounded men and women sitting beside the trail. It was the Indian custom for people who were about to die to leave the tribe and wait for death. This was done voluntarily so as not to be a burden on the rest of the people. In one case a wounded Indian woman asked some soldiers to put her out of her misery. The soldiers refused, but Bannock scouts traveling with the army readily complied with the woman's request.[2]

The second night out, Chief Joseph made camp at Horse Prairie, close to the village of Bannock, Montana. The people of Bannock, afraid of an Indian raid on their village, assembled all available men to assist in their defense. However, the Nez Perce made no attempt to enter the town.

Lone Elk and his braves came across a ranch at the lower end of Horse Prairie. The warriors killed most of the men at the ranch, then ransacked the ranch house looking for bandage material. While the killing of the ranch hands seemed like a wanton act of murder, it must be remembered that the Nez Perce were still bitter over their losses at the Big Hole Basin. They felt betrayed by the settlers after all of their attempts to maintain friendly relations with inhabitants of the Bitterroot Valley. The Indians took all of the horses they could find, feeling that they could always use more horses. In addition, taking the horses prevented the army from getting them.[3]

Howard sent messengers to warn the people of Salmon, Idaho, and the various small communities along the Lemhi River of a possible attack by the Nez Perce. However, no attack was ever made. It should also be noted that at no time did the Nez Perce ever harm women or children, nor did they ever take scalps or mutilate bodies.

On leaving Horse Prairie, Chief Joseph took his people over the Continental Divide and through Bannock Pass into the Idaho Territory. As in the past, their only objective was to avoid the army and reach some place where they could live in peace.

Howard was assured by some scouts, members of the "Treaty Nez Perce" who had joined his command, that the main body of Nez Perce would not head down the Mormon Trail. Their real objective was to re-enter Montana by way of the Clark's Fork

River. Because of this, Howard did not follow directly behind the Nez Perce. Instead he stayed to the north and entered Idaho by way of the Monida Pass. His objective was to intercept the Nez Perce on the Camas Meadow near the present town of Dubois, Idaho.

Chief Joseph led his people east toward the Camas Meadow. As they approached Birch Creek, an advance party of warriors intercepted five freight wagons heading toward Montana. The warriors demanded guns and ammunition from the freighters. Things remained semi-friendly until a barrel of whiskey was found. The warriors soon became drunk and their demands lost all semblance of friendliness. The freighters were killed with the exception of one man who was able to hide in the willow thickets along Birch Creek. The warriors took what they wanted and then burned the wagons and the rest of their contents.[4]

On August 19, Chief Joseph made camp near the Snake River Plain along the edge of Camas Creek. At about the same time, Howard also reached Camas Meadows. Bannock scouts came upon the Nez Perce and shots were fired. While no one was hurt, the Nez Perce were warned that the army was close by. Because of the nearness of the army, the Nez Perce moved their camp about fifteen miles to the north. That night an old Nez Perce warrior had a dream of his people running off with all of Howard's horses. The next day he told the chiefs about his dream. His dream was discussed all that afternoon by the chiefs and elders. Dreams were now taken very seriously after Chief Looking Glass had ignored them back at the Big Hole Basin.

At midnight, Ollikut and about thirty warriors rode toward Howard's camp. They hoped to find the horses grazing randomly over the meadow and very few sentinels guarding them. The scouts, however, observed numerous sentinels and noticed that the horses had been securely tethered, but the mules were free to graze at random. On returning to their camp, Ollikut relayed this information to the chiefs. In spite of the army's precautions, it was decided that the horse raid should be carried out.

The following night the warriors again departed for Howard's camp. The Indians divided into two groups, approaching the camp from opposite sides. The primary group, under the direction of Ollikut, rode as quietly as possible, reaching the edge of the camp a little after three in the morning. Several of the warriors dismounted and crept among the horses cutting the tether ropes, but before Ollikut's raiders had a chance to free many horses, they were spotted by the army sentinels. One of the sentinels called out, "Who goes there?" At the same time one of the Indian raiders accidently fired his rifle, alerting the entire camp.

As soon as their presence was detected, Ollikut and his warriors started shooting. War whoops and screaming caused all of the mules and horses that had been freed to stampede north toward the mountains. Ollikut and his raiders were close behind the animals. For the first six or seven miles they stayed fairly close together, but as soon as they reached the mountains there was a general scattering of all the animals.[5]

A troop of cavalry was now in full pursuit. By the time the cavalry reached the mountain area, the Nez Perce had taken up defensive positions and began firing at the approaching army troops. This kept the army from immediately rounding up the mules and horses. By the time the battle was over, the mules had become so scattered that only a few were recovered.

The battle of Camas Meadow lasted about four hours. The army suffered two killed and five wounded.

The Nez Perce had two warriors slightly wounded. The main result of the battle was to deprive General Howard of his pack animals, thus keeping him from a rapid pursuit of the fleeing Nez Perce.[6]

Chief Joseph was probably aware of the problems the horse and mule raid had caused General Howard. This was shown when he told his people, "Our need for haste is not now as great. While we must not tarry, we can travel at a more relaxed pace." The Nez Perce did not immediately break camp, but spent the afternoon gathering food. They broke camp and left early the next morning. By that night they had reached an area around Henry's Lake. The following day the Nez Perce again crossed the Continental Divide at Targhee Pass and traveled on to the Madison River at the edge of Yellowstone Park.

Chief Joseph knew his people could travel at a faster pace. While some of the wounded had died, most of the others were well on the road to recovery. Very few travoises were now required to transport the wounded who were mostly children.

While General Howard was taking a short cut to Camas Meadow, he had ordered Lieutenant Bacon to take a company of forty cavalrymen and make a forced ride to Targhee Pass, a short distance from Henry's Lake. When Bacon arrived, he sent scouts down to Henry's Lake to see if there were any Nez Perce in the area. Because they were a couple of days ahead of the Nez Perce, none were seen. Bacon decided that the Nez Perce were not coming his way; he immediately vacated the area and went in search of Howard. He and his troops took the wrong route back and missed both the oncoming Indians and Howard.[7]

Chief Joseph was not aware of the error made by Bacon. This mistake allowed the Nez Perce to travel freely into Yellowstone Park.

Chapter 11

Passage Through Yellowstone Park

While Chief Looking Glass was no longer responsible for the defense of the Nez Perce, he was responsible for the route they would take through Yellowstone Park. Yellow Wolf was in charge of the scouts who were alert for any possible danger. Each day these scouts went out in all directions to ensure that no army troops or other hostile forces were in the area.

The Council of Chiefs had decided to travel down the Madison River and then up the Clark's Fork of the Yellowstone River instead of taking the shorter route across the Gallatin range. They hoped to confuse General Howard about where they were going.

The first day in Yellowstone Park, Yellow Wolf and his cousin were on scouting duties when they heard someone chopping wood a short distance away. Dismounting, they crept up and found a man cutting wood for his campfire. Standing up, Yellow Wolf strode up and confronted the camper. "Yo, white man, who are you and what are you doing here?" It turned out that he was a prospector from the Black Hills of South Dakota on his way back to Montana. Yellow Wolf took him back to the chiefs, who gave him a horse and treated him in a very friendly manner. It was hoped that the prospector had good knowledge of Yellowstone Park and could act as a guide. Apparently the treatment he received met with his satisfaction, since he stayed with the Nez Perce for about a week.[1]

While the Nez Perce were starting through Yellowstone Park, Howard had made a forced march to Henry's Lake. When he learned that Lieutenant Bacon had left his post, allowing the Nez Perce to travel on to Yellowstone Park without interference, the general wanted to move on as rapidly as possible in pursuit. However, his chief medical officer, along with several other officers, strongly advised that the troops were too worn out to be effective in any potential battle with the Nez Perce. They argued that the troops should be allowed to rest, and General Howard finally agreed.

While the troops were resting, two things of interest happened. A group of Bannock warriors recruited from Fort Hall could not understand the reason for the delay or why the white man got so tired. After about three days, they became so disgusted that a few started leaving for home. At the same time, Howard took a small group on a forced march to Virginia City, Montana, about sixty miles away. Here he sent a wire to General Sherman, explaining the condition of his men and the reason for the delay. However, Sherman came to the wrong conclusion about the wire. He immediately sent a wire back to Howard that in essence said, "If you aren't young and vigorous enough to keep up with the Indians, then maybe you should select a younger person as your replacement." As one can imagine, this didn't put Howard in the best of spirits. This wire was followed by several wires going back and forth. Howard was telling Sherman that he could keep up with any officer in his command. Sherman began back peddling telling Howard that he was sorry for the apparent misinterpretation of what he really meant.[2]

While Howard was having his problems with Sherman, the troops he had brought with him were busy buying horses, mules and other needed supplies. They had brought many worn-out horses with them to either sell or trade, if at all possible. These troops did buy many horses, but they also got a very unpleasant surprise. When they tried to saddle them, they found that most of the horses had never been broken. The sergeant in charge went to Howard and said, "General, we have shore been taken by these goldurn ranchers. Most of those broncs have never been ridden. When we get back to Henry's Lake we are going to have one of the goldurndest bronc-bustin events you've ever seen if we're ever going to use them animals." General Howard decided to keep the horses and break them only if and when they were needed.

Howard again made a forced march back to his troops at Henry's Lake. With a good four days rest, the troops were ready to go. The following day, they entered the west entrance to Yellowstone Park.[3]

Yellowstone Park had been established about five years earlier in March, 1872. At that time there were no roads or camping facilities. People could camp wherever they desired and hunt and fish all they wanted. The only mode of travel was either on foot or on horseback. In spite of these inconveniences, the park had about five hundred visitors a year.[4]

When Howard entered Yellowstone Park, he again had to rely on the Idaho volunteers to make a road for the wagons and pack animals. The Nez Perce did not have this problem. They were able to go wherever they wanted on horseback.

The first night in the park, the Nez Perce camped on the banks of the Firehole River. A group of visitors from Montana, camped a short distance away, were not aware of the Indian presence. The following morning they were surprised to see several Indians entering their camp. One of the braves strode forward and said, "We come in peace. We want coffee and bacon. We will pay for what we get." One of the visitors refused, which did not please the Indians at all. This caused a heated argument between the Indians and the Montana visitors. The final result was that the Indians took the white visitors as prisoners. The visitors asked to be taken to the Nez Perce chiefs to see if they could negotiate their freedom. Among the visitors were two white women who were very scared of the treatment they might receive.

At the main Indian camp a council of chiefs was held. The decision of the chiefs was relayed to the visitors by Chief Looking Glass. This message contained the basic philosophy of the Nez Perce when he said, "The white man has killed many of our women and children. The Nez Perce do not make war on women and children. We do not make war on the people of Montana. We will give you horses without saddles and you are free to leave. When you leave, you will not spy on us."

The Montana visitors mounted their horses and started on the back trail. About two miles from camp, two of the white men dismounted and ducked into the brush. Indian scouts who had been following saw the two men leave. They immediately stopped the rest of the party and demanded the other two men. The Montanans expressed ignorance about their absence. When there was no apparent cooperation, one of the Indians fired, hitting a visitor in the leg. Another shot hit a white visitor in the face. His wife immediately jumped from her horse and held her husband's head. She was dragged away and the man was again shot in the head and left there for dead. At this point some of the chiefs arrived and put an end to the shooting. The man who had been shot in the head was not dead. He lay on the ground unconscious until after dark. When he awoke, he started crawling to their old camp at Lower Geyser Basin, about nine miles away. About four days later he finally reached his destination. All food had been removed, but he was able to find some matches with which to build a welcome fire.[5]

On the following day, two of Howard's scouts came by and found him. "Who are you and what happened to you?" one of the scouts demanded.

"I'm George Cowan," replied the wounded man. There was a stunned silence.

"We done heard you was dead and we've come up here to bury you," said one of the scouts. George Cowan was taken back to Howard, where the army doctors took care of him. He made a full recovery.

When the Nez Perce left George Cowan for dead, the remaining white visitors were taken back to the Indian village and kept prisoners for the next twenty-four hours. During the night, the two white women stayed by the campfire of Chief Joseph. While he did not talk, they were very impressed with his dignity. Their impression of most of the Nez Perce was that they were a very light-hearted and happy people.

Chief Joseph was not in a talking mood. He had felt that when they reached Montana their war would be over. Now it appeared that they would be followed until they were defeated. He was also concerned about how much longer the women and old men could keep traveling. Their clothes were becoming worn, and some did not have blankets or robes to cover them at night. He also wondered if the army could follow them after they reentered Montana. Would they continue to follow after they entered Canada? There were many problems and he did not have the answers.

As they traveled through the park, the majority of Nez Perce proceeded in a peaceful manner. However, a small group of renegades went on raiding trips throughout the area. Visitors to the park were being shot. Ranches were being burned, and a general state of fear existed throughout the region.

Howard was still trying to catch up with the Nez Perce but making very slow time. On several occasions, the Bannock scouts who got within earshot of the Nez Perce informed General Howard of the Nez Perce presence, but couldn't get the general to move any faster. Because of this, more of the Bannock scouts deserted and returned to their homes at Fort Hall.[6]

The Nez Perce were still trying to find the best way out of Yellowstone Park and back into Montana. Yellow Wolf and his scouts found that the three main routes out of the Park were being guarded. They reported to the chiefs that Colonel Sturgis was on the Clark's Fork of the Yellowstone River, Major Hart was guarding the Shoshone River, and General Merritt was on the Wind River at the south entrance to the Park. In addition, Captain Cushing was near the Crow Agency located northeast of the Park.

The break for the Nez Perce came when scouting parties for Sturgis reported no signs of the Nez Perce. Like Lieutenant Bacon at Targhee Pass, the scouts were a couple of days too early to encounter the Nez Perce. Based on this lack of information, Sturgis became convinced that the Nez Perce were heading for the Shoshone River Pass to make their way into Montana. On this basis, he broke camp and headed for that area. His decision was further reinforced when Lieutenant Fuller and a guide got a glimpse of an Indian column heading toward the Shoshone River exit. The guide with Fuller told Sturgis that there was no available pass that far south the Indians could take to reach the Clark's Fork River. It never occured to Sturgis that the Nez Perce might retrace their steps and take the Clark's Fork route. This, in fact, is what they did. About two days after Sturgis left his position, the Nez Perce went over the Clark's Fork Pass without encountering a single soldier.[7]

Chapter 12

Trails Across Montana

Chief Joseph immediately started his people up the Clark's Fork River toward the Yellowstone River valley. The general direction was north toward Canada. Chief Joseph agreed with the other chiefs that no time should be wasted. This was shown when he told his people, "We must hurry while the weather lasts and put as much distance as possible between us and the army. It is apparent the army will keep following and not let us rest."

It took Colonel Sturgis about two days to realize the error he had made. His scouts had picked up the trail of the Nez Perce where they had come across the Clark's Fork pass. Sturgis immediately returned to the area. There he met General Howard just emerging from Yellowstone Park.

Howard was the first to speak, "Colonel, my scouts tell me that the Nez Perce took the Clark's Fork route back into Montana. You had orders to guard this pass. Explain to me what happened."

Sturgis paused for a minute trying to collect the words that would put this military error in a better light. Finally he said, "General, my scouts assured me that the Nez Perce were heading toward the Shoshone River pass. From where they were last seen, there was no way they could have reached the Clark's Fork River trail. Based on this information, I proceeded to the Shoshone River Pass to assist Major Hart when those Indians came through." After the initial exchange, the two officers retired to General Howard's tent to discuss what had happened. They were both very chagrined by how the Nez Perce had fooled them. They had also gained a great deal of respect for the Nez Perce leaders. One of the first things the two officers did was send a message to Fort Keogh on the Tongue River at the site of present-day Miles City, Montana.

Howard instructed his aide to find one of his scouts and bring him to the tent. It wasn't long before Sam Fisher, one of his best scouts arrived. Sam had been raised and had trapped throughout the Idaho-Montana area and knew the country like the back of his hand. He looked and smelled like a typical scout. His long braided hair fell down over his shoulders. His buckskin blouse and pants were worn and dirty, showing the effects of many days in the saddle and Sam's reluctance to wash or take a bath. However, he knew every trail and path in the area and had an uncanny sense of direction. There was no danger of him ever getting lost.

When Howard looked up, he said, "Hello, Sam, I've got a message I want you to deliver. I want you to take this letter to Colonel Miles and deliver it to him personally. I don't want some aide to take it and lose it."

Sam gave Howard a sleepy look and said, "I suppose this here colonel is still located at Fort Keogh. There ain't no place in Montana I can't find, and Fort Keogh I could find blindfolded." After a short pause he added, "How soon do you want this here piece of

General Nelson A. Miles
(Montana Historical Society Research Center)

paper delivered? I can be there in two days or sooner if you want."

Howard had known Sam Fisher for many years and couldn't repress a smile at his well-known nonchalant attitude. He ended the meeting with these instructions, "Sam, I want this message in the Colonel's hand as soon as possible. Don't stop at some Crow or Blackfoot camp to visit for a few days."

The message Sam carried was a request for Colonel Nelson A. Miles to try and intercept the Nez Perce and hold them until Howard and Sturgis could catch up.

Both Howard and Sturgis were anxious to redeem themselves from the errors they had made. It was decided to pursue the Nez Perce as rapidly as possible. Sturgis' men and horses were more rested and in better condition to travel than those of Howard; therefore, Sturgis was given permission to take the lead in their relentless pursuit.

It was now the middle of September, and the weather was starting to make the change toward winter. The first day Colonel Sturgis and his men covered about sixty miles in a heavy rainstorm. While the rain had not yet turned to snow, the nights were getting colder. There was usually a thin coating of ice on the water in the morning. It was uncomfortable for the soldiers with all of their equipment, but it was plain miserable for the Indians who had lost most of their possessions at the Big Hole Battle Ground.[1] It is rather ironic to note that when Sturgis called a halt at the end of the day's march, they were within a few miles of the Nez Perce.

Upon reaching the Yellowstone River valley, Chief Looking Glass went in search of his friends in the Crow Nation. He was able to find them, but was shocked and disappointed when they refused to help and declared themselves strictly neutral. Again, the Nez Perce found they were on their own. In spite of all these problems, the stature of Chief Joseph was steadily growing among all the Nez Perce people. This was due to his continual concern for the well being of everyone regardless of tribal affiliation. On the other hand, Chief Looking Glass was losing a lot of respect due to his tactical errors prior to the Big Hole Battle and to the uncooperative attitude of the Crow people after all of his bragging about his friends in the Crow Nation.

Chief Joseph was leisurely leading his people toward Canyon Creek, north of the Yellowstone River, when he saw a scout sending a signal with a blanket from a distant hillside. The signal meant that soldiers were coming up rapidly from behind. On seeing the signal, the main body of Nez Perce made a run for the canyon entrance. At the same time Yellow Wolf and Ollikut, with a party of braves, found protective cover behind boulders and fallen logs. When the charging cavalry came within range, the Nez Perce opened fire. The amount and accuracy of the fire power caused the cavalry to dismount and proceed on foot. This tactic allowed the Indian rear guard to withdraw slowly while the main body of Nez Perce was getting away.[2]

The conduct of the Canyon Creek battle by Sturgis proved to be his second major mistake. The colonel assumed that the Nez Perce would dig in and fight a battle with his troops. This was not the case. The Nez Perce warriors were merely trying to slow the army down so that the main body of people could make their escape. As the army slowed down, the Nez Perce warriors slowly withdrew, guarding the rear from any possible attack. As in previous battles, Nez Perce marksmanship was much superior to that of the army. Sturgis had three soldiers killed and eleven wounded. The Nez Perce claimed that only three warriors were wounded.

Sturgis camped at Canyon Creek battle ground until Howard arrived. Once again supplied, he took to the field in pursuit of the Nez Perce. During the next three days, the cavalry traveled approximately 150 miles. This brought them to the Musselshell River, a tributary of the Missouri River. At this point, Sturgis decided that he could not overtake or keep up with the Nez Perce. His men and horses were so worn out that they would have been completely ineffective in battle. Therefore, he made camp and waited for Howard to catch up.

While the army was having difficulty keeping up with the Nez Perce, the Bannock and Crow scouts were having a great time! They continually harassed the Nez Perce, with the primary objective of stealing horses. To some extent they were successful, but the Nez Perce were able to protect the majority of their horses from capture.[3]

When Sturgis stopped at the Musselshell River, Chief Joseph and the other chiefs felt that their worries with the army were over. They were not aware that Miles from Fort Keogh was also starting out after them.

The rapid pace the Nez Perce were maintaining had an effect primarily on the elderly, some of whom were beginning to fall by the wayside. The rapid pace during the day, along with the cold and damp climate at night, was more than some of them could endure. It is a tribute to Chief Joseph's leadership that he was able to keep his people moving at such a pace.

The Nez Perce were trying to reach Cow Island on the Missouri River as rapidly as possible. In the late fall, Cow Island became the head of navigation on the Missouri River. It was also the supply station for the forts and settlements of northern Montana and even some of the frontier posts in Canada. A river boat had left supplies for Fort Benton, with a detachment of about a dozen soldiers who remained there as guards. The soldiers had received word that the Nez Perce were heading in their direction, so they had built breastworks around the area for their protection.

When the Nez Perce arrived in the area, they swam their horses across the Missouri River and established a camp a few miles from the barricaded soldiers. In the meantime, a group of warriors remained behind and asked for a meeting with the leader of the soldiers. When he appeared, an older warrior named Yellow Hawk said, "We come in peace. We do not want to harm you. My people are hungry and cold; we want food and clothing for them. We have money and we will pay for what we get."

The request was refused. However, the army spokesman said, "If you will surrender, we will give you food for your people and blankets to keep them warm."[4]

Needless to say, the Nez Perce did not feel that this was a good arrangement. At this point there was a short exchange of gunfire. One Indian and two soldiers were wounded. The Nez Perce then took what they needed and burned the rest of the supplies. They later defended their action on the grounds that the supplies were going to the army. Since this was war, they felt anything that would hurt the army was justified.

The following morning the Nez Perce left on their journey north. At the same time, a detachment of troops under Major Ilges arrived at Cow Island from Fort Benton. When he saw what had happened, he decided to pursue the Nez Perce. By noon he had overtaken the Nez Perce but was surprised to find that the Indians had encountered a freight wagon. Three of the teamsters had been killed, and the warriors were going through the supplies, taking whatever could be of use to them. They were now burning the wagons and unneeded supplies. Ilges attacked the Indians, but when one of his men was killed, he decided it best to withdraw and return to Cow Island.

About this time the Nez Perce made a very crucial error. Lean Elk, leader of the caravan, was in favor of a continued rapid pace into Canada. Looking Glass was in favor of a much slower pace. They now had supplies and game was much more plentiful. The weather was becoming miserable, and the people as well as the horses were exhausted. Above all, they still did not know that Miles was on his way to intercept them. Based on these conditions, Chief Looking Glass replaced Lean Elk as the caravan leader. The Nez Perce proceeded a short distance farther and made camp at the Bears Paw Mountains. It was their intent to rest here for a few days and then move on at a leisurely pace on into Canada, only about forty miles away.

Chapter 13

Final Battle at Bears Paw Mountain

On September 18, just one day after receiving orders from General Howard, Colonel Miles was ready to move out against the Nez Perce. From Howard's letter he had a vague idea about the general direction the Nez Perce were taking and where they possibly could be found. With this information he set a direct course for Cow Island on the Missouri River. When Miles reached the Missouri River, he was lucky enough to encounter a steamboat. This boat, the last of the season, ferried half of his command across the river.

It was his intention to proceed up both sides of the river just in case the Nez Perce had not yet crossed.

Within an hour of Miles releasing the steamboat, a messenger arrived from Cow Island with the news that the Nez Perce had crossed and were proceeding north toward Canada. Miles was able to overtake the steamboat and have it return to ferry the rest of his troops to the north side of the river.[1]

Four days later, a group of Cheyenne scouts working with Miles discovered the trail of the Nez Perce. By all signs, they were not very far ahead. A message was sent to Miles who rapidly brought his forces forward. He came within sight of the Nez Perce encampment on the early morning of September 30th.

Miles had made every effort to overtake the Nez Perce as rapidly as possible. He was very ambitious, with a strong desire to make general. He knew that a successful battle with the Nez Perce would gain him national recognition, and probably the promotion he desired. His first task was to beat the Nez Perce before Howard could arrive. He had no desire to share the glory with his superior.

Lone Wolf had sent out scouts the day before, but no sign of any troops could be found. It was also observed that herds of buffalo, elk and antelope were quietly grazing on the prairie, a further indication that army personnel were not in the area. Based on this information, the Nez Perce did not send out any scouts or sentinels.[2]

Miles' first assessment of the Indian encampment was that everyone was still sleeping. However, an army scout soon observed a sudden spurt of activity. He immediately rode back and found Miles and delivered this message, "Colonel, them Indians shore must know about us being here as they are jumping out of their tepees like ants out of an ant hill."

Miles assumed that some early morning hunter had spotted the army's presence and sounded a warning. There appeared to be no time for a detailed planning of the attack.

The Nez Perce camp was located in a small cove next to Snake Creek. Miles developed a three-pronged attack. One column was to come in from the left, another column was to come in from the right, while a third column was to make a frontal attack. When the troops came within a hundred yards, the Nez Perce opened fire. Captain Carter, who was leading the frontal attack, brought his command up to the edge of the Indian village but had to withdraw when over half of his command was killed.

At the very start of the battle, Chief Joseph raced to the horse herd and grabbed a mount for his daughter Kapkap Pomme, which in English translates into Sound of Running Feet. "Kapkap Pomme, take this horse and join our people who are fleeing north." With these few words, she was sent north with Chief White Bird and about 150 other Nez Perce who were making a final dash to Canada. On parting, he also told his daughter he had to return to her mother and the other children. Chief Joseph made a miraculous dash back to the village through the army troops. He later said there were guns firing on all sides with bullets passing all around him. He made it back to his tepee unharmed. His wife met him at their lodge, handed him his rifle and told him to go fight.[3]

The day had dawned clear and cold with no breeze stirring the air. Under these conditions, the air was soon filled with the white cloud of gun smoke. All around was the screaming of the wounded mixed with the yelling and whoops of the army and Nez Perce.

Again, the accuracy of the Nez Perce rifle fire was superior to that of the army. It didn't take Miles very long to decide that attacks by the cavalry were not going to be very successful. They were losing too many troops. The only possible way to beat the Nez Perce was to dig in for an extended siege. While these plans were being carried out, a message was sent back to Howard requesting that he proceed with all haste with his reinforcements.

The Nez Perce warriors were rapidly digging trenches and foxholes for protection of themselves and their families. The women and children who had been unable or unwilling to try an escape to Canada were assisting their men in every way they possibly could. Most of the Nez Perce who were killed met their death on the first day of battle. These included such familiar names as Lean Elk, Ollikut, Pile of Clouds and Too hool hool zote.[4]

When the supply wagons arrived with the howitzer, it was immediately put into action. It was soon found that the gun was useless unless the barrel could be elevated. This was because the Nez Perce were dug in below a small hill. In order for the shells to reach them, the barrel of the howitzer would have to be pointed up into the air. This would allow the shells to travel up and over the hill and drop down onto the Indian emplacements. This was accomplished by digging the tongue of the howitzer down into the ground. After a couple of adjustments, the shells were hitting around the Nez Perce with remarkable accuracy.[5]

As in previous battles, the Nez Perce fought with ferocious intensity. Because there were few warriors remaining, the survivors could not afford the luxury of sleep. The only sleep possible was short naps for a few of the warriors while the others kept watch. In addition, fires could not be lit for either cooking or warmth, as the light from the fire would make easy targets for the army. The only food available was dried meat. To add to their misery, a cold wind was blowing and a snow storm was developing. At the end of the second day the ground was covered with a blanket of snow. Each morning the shelling resumed. The Nez Perce returned the fire as rapidly and accurately as they could, but by the end of the third day of battle, Chief Joseph could see they were fighting a losing cause.

Chief Joseph had asked Chief White Bird to find Chief Sitting Bull, who had escaped to Canada after the battle at the Little Big Horn. Chief White Bird was to request that the Sioux come to the aid of the Nez Perce at the Bears Paw. Chief White Bird found Chief Sitting Bull but he refused to help. He did not want to alienate himself or his people any further with the white leaders in case they ever wanted to return to the United States. This was only one year after the battle at the Little Big Horn and the army was still a little upset over the beating they had taken. In addition to refusing, Chief Sitting Bull moved his people many miles farther away from the border.[6]

On about the third day of battle, the Nez Perce could see a large group of dark shapes moving through the snow. They were convinced that these shapes were the Sioux coming to their aid. However, their elation was soon dispelled when it was determined that the shapes were a herd of buffalo trying to find protection from the storm.

At about that same time, Chief Looking Glass observed a mounted warrior riding toward them. He assumed that this was a messenger sent from Chief Sitting Bull. When Chief Looking Glass rose for a better view of the warrior, a bullet struck him in the forehead. His death was instantaneous.

Chief Looking Glass was the fifth chief to be killed at the battle of the Bears Paw. With his death, Chief Joseph realized that the Nez Perce could no longer exist as they had in the past. Most of the tribal leaders were now dead. The tribal groups that had existed were no longer there.[7]

On the evening of October 4, Howard arrived at the Bears Paw battle scene. He was welcomed with military courtesy by Miles and his aides. While Miles was glad to see the reinforcements, he was not thrilled with the presence of Howard. In spite of the long campaign of Howard, Miles felt he deserved most of the credit for defeating the Nez Perce. The reserved feeling lasted until Howard sent his aide to invite Miles to his tent for a meeting. On his arrival, Howard said, "Colonel you have brought about a victory that we have been unable to attain in about four months of fighting. Because of your accomplishment, you are directed to take the lead in any peace negotiations that should be coming in the very near future." When Miles found he was to be the lead peace negotiator, he became quite friendly and agreeable. After a short discussion, both Howard and Miles agreed that the Nez Perce had fought honorably and fairly during the entire campaign and should be treated with dignity and respect.

Shortly after the meeting with General Howard, a messenger under a white flag was sent to summon Chief Joseph to a meeting where the terms of surrender would be discussed. During this meeting Chief Joseph was assured that most of their rifles and horses would be returned to them. He was also told that his people would be taken to Fort Keogh where they would be fed and sheltered until the following spring. At that time, they would be returned to the reservation at Lapwai, Idaho. At this point Chief Joseph said, "General you have known me for many moons. You know that my heart is pure and that what I say is true. I will take your message back to my people and discuss what you have proposed. I will return as soon as I can with their decision. I have one request that I will make of you. Many of my people are scattered across the prairie toward Canada and into the surrounding mountains. I want to gather and save as many as I can find that are still alive and bring them back with me"

On the morning of October 5, another messenger arrived at the Indian encampment. He

Chief Joseph
(Library of Congress)

brought the message that the army was getting impatient for the Nez Perce decision. Chief Joseph sent back word that they were not yet ready. That afternoon, Chief Joseph sent a message to tell Howard that his people had agreed to the terms and he was ready to surrender his rifle.

A buffalo robe was placed on the ground at a point midway between the army and the Indian camp. Howard and Miles approached the robe from the army side, while Chief Joseph approached from the Indian camp. When the two sides met, Chief Joseph handed his rifle toward Howard. The general refused the rifle and directed Chief Joseph to Miles. When Miles received the rifle, Chief Joseph stepped back and delivered these now famous words:

> "Tell General Howard I know his heart. What he told me before I have in my heart. I am tired of fighting. Our chiefs are killed. Looking Glass is dead. The old men are all killed. It is the young men who say yes or no. He who led the young men is dead. It is cold and we have no blankets. The little children are freezing to death. My people, some of them, have run away to the hills

and have no blankets, no food; no one knows where they are, perhaps freezing to death. I want time to look for my children and see how many of them I can find. Maybe I shall find them among the dead. Hear me, my chiefs, I am tired, my heart is sick and sad. From where the sun now stands, I will fight no more forever."

EPILOGUE

The Nez Perce War

Seldom Heard Facts

The Nez Perce War started at White Bird, Idaho, on June 17, 1877, and ended at the Bears Paw Mountains in Montana on October 5, 1877. During this 111-day period, the Nez Perce traveled over 1500 miles, and engaged ten separate U.S. Commands in thirteen different battles. In nearly every case the Nez Perce either defeated the army or fought them to a draw. In addition, in every battle, the Nez Perce were heavily outnumbered. For example, at White Bird there were seventy Nez Perce warriors facing 100 soldiers. At the end of the battle, thirty-four soldiers were killed, while only two Nez Perce warriors were wounded.

Another extraordinary fact was the number and mix of the Nez Perce. At the Clearwater River, the bands of Chief Joseph, Chief White Bird, and Too hool hool zote were joined by those of Chief Looking Glass and Red Echo. The combined groups now totaled about 700 people. Of this number, only about 150 men were of fighting age while the remaining 550 were older men, women and children. In addition to all of the people, they were herding about 2,000 to 3,000 head of horses and cattle. Even though the army had only soldiers and pack animals, they were unable to keep up with the Nez Perce. As noted above, the Nez Perce started over the Lolo Trail with about 700 people. At the end of the final battle, the Nez Perce were down to about 430 people, with only 79 fighting men remaining.

It should also be noted that the Nez Perce did not initiate any battle, with the possible exception of the battle at Camas Meadows. At this battle, their only objective was to scatter General Howard's horses and pack mules to delay his pursuit. The only objective the Nez Perce had during the entire war was to avoid the army and find a place where they could live in peace.

Aftermath of the War

It was Chief Joseph's understanding when he surrendered following the battle at the Bears Paw Mountains, that he and his people would be taken to Fort Keogh and held until the following spring. As soon as the passes were clear of snow, they would be returned to their reservation at Lapwai, Idaho. This is exactly what General Howard and Colonel Miles intended to do. However, their superior, General William Tecumseh Sherman, Chief of the Armies, changed the order. He felt that the Nez Perce should be treated with severity and never be allowed to return to their native areas in Idaho and Oregon.

Late that fall, the remaining Nez Perce were crowded aboard a train and sent to Fort Leavenworth, Kansas. During the winter, about twenty died of malaria. The following spring the Nez Perce were moved to the Quapaw reservation in Kansas where they stayed for one month. They were then relocated to another Kansas reservation. By fall about forty-seven more Nez Perce had perished. During October, 1878, Chief Joseph was granted permission to travel to Washington, D.C., to present his case to the law makers. He also gave public interviews. In 1879, Chief Joseph addressed Congress and gave one of his most famous speeches, which can be found in "Quotes from Chief Joseph" Nez Perce National Historical Park, Lapwai, Idaho.

"I cannot understand how the Government sends men out tofight us, as did General Miles, and then breaks his word. Such a Government has something wrong with it. I cannot understand why so many chiefs are allowed to talk so many different ways, and promise so many different things. I have seen the Great White Father (the President); the next great chief (Secretary of the Interior); the Commissioner Chief (Hayt); the Law Chief (General Butler); and many other

Chief Joseph, Peo Peo Tah Likt, and Stephen Reuben,
Nez Perce Delegation to Washington, D.C., 1900
(Dept. of Interior, Nez Perce National Historical Park)

law chiefs (Congressmen) and they all say they are my friend, and that I shall have justice, but while their mouths all talk right, I do not understand why nothing is done for my people. I have heard talk and talk but nothing is done. Good words do not last long if they do not amount to something. Words do not pay for my dead people. They do not pay for my country, now overrun by white men. They do not protect my father's grave. They do not pay for my horses and cattle. Good words will not make good the promises of your War Chief, General Miles. Good words will not give my people good health and stop them from dying. Good words will not get my people a home where they can live in peace and take care of themselves. I am tired of talk that comes to nothing. It makes my heart sick when I remember all the good words and all the broken promises. There has been too much talking by men who have no right to talk. Too many misrepresentations have been

Pile of Clouds and Wife of Cloud the Elder
(Dept. of Interior, Nez Perce National Historical Park)

made. Too many misunderstandings have come up between white men about the Indians. If the white man wants to live in peace with the Indians, he can live in peace. There need be no trouble. Treat all men alike. Give them all the same law. Give them all the same chance to live and grow. All men were made by the Great Spirit Chief. They are all brothers. The earth is the mother of all people, and all people should have equal rights upon it. You might as well expect the river to run backwards as that any man who was born free should be content penned up and denied liberty to go where he pleases. If you tie a horse to a stake do you expect he will grow fat? If you pen an Indian up on a small spot of earth, and compel him to stay there, he will not be content, nor will he grow and prosper. I have asked some of the great white chiefs where they got their authority to say to the Indian that he shall stay in one place, while he sees the white men going where they

please. They cannot tell me. Whenever the
white man treats the Indian as he treats
each other, then we shall have no more
wars. We shall all be alike, brother of one
father and one mother, with one sky
above us and one country around us, and
one government for all. The Great Spirit
Chief who rules above will smile upon
this land and send rain to wash out the
bloody spots made by brothers' hands
upon the face of the earth. For this time
the Indian race is waiting and praying."

By 1883 the plight of the Nez Perce had gained
national attention and sympathy. Washington decided
that it would be to their political advantage to let them
return to the Northwest. During May of 1885, the
surviving Nez Perce boarded a train for home. There
were now 268 remaining of the 700 who had started
over the Lolo Trail.

The Nez Perce problem was not completely
over. Of the 268 remaining Nez Perce, only 118 were
allowed to return to the Lapwai reservation. The other
150, including Chief Joseph, were sent to the Colville

reservation in the Washington Territory. Chief Joseph was still considered too dangerous to be returned to Lapwai.

Chief Joseph spent the rest of his life trying to better the conditions of his people. In particular, Joseph wanted to return to Wallowa to the land he loved and to be near the graves of his father and his mother.

For Chief Joseph the end came on the evening of September 21, 1904. While seated by the fire in his tepee, he had a massive heart attack and died, never having been allowed to live again in his beloved Wallowa Valley.

Nez Perce Encampment at Lapwai, Idaho, July 4, 1911
(Dept. of Interior, Nez Perce National Historical Park)

Of interest is a current development quoted in a July 1996 issue of the *New York Times*. According to this newspaper account, the people of Joseph, Wallowa and Enterprise, Oregon, are actively seeking the return of the Nez Perce people. This is based strictly on economic considerations. Lumbering and ranching, which had been the mainstay of their economy, have fallen on hard times. The biggest attractions in the area are the historical sites of the Nez Perce and in particular the grave of Old Chief Joseph. The white population feel that the development of a Nez Perce cultural and interpretive center would be an economic boon to the area. The Bonneville Power Authority is considering the purchase of 10,000 acres along the stream where young Joseph was born and would donate it to the Nez Perce for hunting and fishing rights.

Many of the Nez Perce feel it is ironic that the white man should now seek their help in preserving the land from which they had been kicked off. If they return, it will be more as a homecoming with deep religious significance, rather than an aid to the white man.

Many of these proposals and developments are now underway. The Bonneville Power Authority has purchased the 10,000 acres along Joseph Creek, about an hour's drive north and east of Enterprise, Oregon. The land was not donated to the Nez Perce as a hunting and fishing preserve, however, but is being run by the Nez Perce as a natural wildlife habitat.

The National Park Service is developing six National Park sites. Only the first one mentioned below has been fully developed.

1. Old Chief Joseph's grave and cemetery. About 1940, the Umatilla Civilian Conservation Corp (CCC) built a rock wall around the cemetery and beautified the site.

2. Dug Bar on the Snake River, the point where Chief Joseph and his people crossed in 1877. This site is located about 53 miles upriver from Lewiston, Idaho.

3. Joseph Canyon Overlook. This is merely a view point overlooking Joseph Creek and the deep canyon where young Joseph

and his family spent many of their winters.

4. A Nez Perce encampment site at the junction of the Lostine and Wallowa Rivers. This site is considered the traditional summer home of the Nez Perce people.

5. A visitors interpretive center at Tick Hill in the Nez Perce homeland. A local oranization with the lengthy title of "Wallowa Band Nez Perce Trail Interpretive Center, Inc.," has acquired 320 acres of land at Tick Hill. This land is dedicated for use by the Nez Perce as an encampment where they can hold powwows and "Pam Ka Liks," which in general means celebration of life.

6. A historical marker will be placed at the top of Minam Grade. This is considered the western gateway to the Wallowa country and the Nez Perce homeland.

The Nez Perce encampments are being used, and many Nez Perce are returning to the Wallowa Valley for visits, but there is not a mad rush to return permanently. While Chief Joseph lived, he wanted to return to the Wallowa Valley to be near the graves of his father and mother. The Nez Perce on the Colville Reservation are several generations removed from that period. Their relatives are buried at that location and they have the same feeling about leaving those graves. In addition, they have very little desire to be put on public display. Like Chief Joseph, their only desire is to live in peace with the white man.

CHAPTER NOTES

Chapter 1. Start of the Nez Perce Discontent

1. Time Life Books, *The Pioneers*, New York, NY, 1974, pp. 17-25
2. Ibid., p, 25
3. David Lavender, *Let Me Be Free*, Harper Collins Press, New York, NY, 1992, p. 144
4. Ibid., p. 147

Chapter 2. Trip to Wallla Walla

1. Bill Gulick, *Chief Joseph Country*,The Caxton Printers, Ltd., Caldwell, ID, 1981, p. 98

Chapter 3. The Treaty of 1855

1. Merrill D. Beal, *I Will Fight No More Forever*, University of Washington Press, Seattle, WA, 1963, P. 25
2. Ibid., pp. 250-253
3. David Lavender, *Let Me Be Free*, Harper Collins Publishers, New York, NY, 1992, p. 176
4. Bill Gulick, *Chief Joseph Country*, Caxton Printers, Ltd., Caldwell, ID, 1981, pp. 97-98
5. Lavender, p. 149
6. Ibid., pp. 149-150
7. Beal, p. 26

Chapter 4. Years of Turmoil

    1. Merrill D. Beal, *I Will Fight No More Forever*, University of Washington Press, Seattle, WA, 1963, P, 28

    2. Ibid., pp. 27-28

    3. Ibid., pp. 30-31

    4. Ibid., pp. 32-33

Chapter 5. Young Chief Joseph

    1. Chief Joseph, *An Indian's View of Indian Affairs*, North American Review, Vol. CXXVIII, April, 1879, p.419

    2. Merrill D. Beal, *I Will Fight No More Forever*, University of Washington Press, Seattle, WA, 1963, P.36

    3. David Lavender, *Let Me Be Free*, Harper Collins Publishers, New York, NY, 1992, pp. 204-205

    4. O. O. Howard, *Nez Perce Joseph*, Boston: Lee and Shephard, 1881, pp. 64-65

    5. Nez Perce Plant Use, Nez Perce Historical Park, Lapwai, Idaho.

    6. Beal, p. 46

Chapter 6. Start of the Nez Perce War

    1. O. O. Howard.*Nez Perce Joseph*. Boston: Lee and Shephard, 1881, p. 99

    2. Merrill D. Beal, *I Will Fight No More Forever*, University of Washington Press, Seattle WA,1963, P. 55

    3.Bill Gulick, *Chief Joseph Country*, Caxton Printers, Caldwell, ID, 1981, pp. 209-210

    4. Beal, p. 58

    5. Gulick, p.211

    6. Beal, pp.65-66

Chapter 7. Escape to the Clearwater

1. Merrill D. Beal, *I Will Fight No More Forever*, University of Washington Press, Seattle, WA, 1963, P.67
2. Bill Gulick, *Chief Joseph Country*, Caxton Printers Ltd., Caldwell, ID, 1981, p. 215
3. Beal, pp. 70-71
4. David Lavender, *Let Me Be Free*, Harper Collins Publishers, New York, NY, 1992, pp.264-265
5. Beal, p. 77

Chapter 8. Trail to Montana

1. Merrill D. Beal, *I Will Fight No More Forever*, University of Washington Press,1963, pp. 79-80
2. Ibid., pp. 83-84
3. Ibid., p. 86
4. Bill Gulick, *Chief Joseph Country*, Caxton Printers, Ltd., Caldwell, ID. 228-230
5. Ibid., p. 231
6. L. V. McWhorter, *Yellow Wolf, His Own Story*, Caxton Printers Ltd., Caldwell, ID, 1940, p. 109

Chapter 9. Battle At The Big Hole Basin

1. Merrill D. Beal, *I Will Fight No More Forever*, University of Washington Press, Seattle, WA,1963, P.88
2. Ibid., p.107
3. Ibid., pp. 109-110
4. David Lavender, *Let Me Be Free*, Harper Collins Publishers, New York, NY, 1992, p. 281
5. Beal, p.117
6. L. V. McWhorter, *Yellow Wolf, His Own Story*, Caxton Printers, Ltd., Caldwell, ID, 1940, p.151

7. Beal, p. 124

Chapter 10. Escape to Yellowstone Park

1. Merrill D. Beal, *I Will Fight No More Forever*, University of Washington Press, Seattle, WA, 1963, pp. 126-127

2. Ibid., p. 130

3. Ibid., p. 145

4. O. O. Howard, *Nez Perce Joseph*, Boston: Lee And Shephard, 1991, p. 203

5. David Lavender, *Let Me Be Free*, Harper Collins Publishers, New York, NY, 1992, pp. 292-293

6. L. V. McWhorter, *Yellow Wolf, His Own Story*, Caxton Ltd., Caldwell, ID, 1940, p. 169

7. Beal, p.163

Chapter 11. Passge Through Yellowstone Park

1. Bill Gulick, *Chief Joseph Country*, Caxton Printers, Ltd. Caldwell, ID, 1981, p. 251

2. Merrill D. Beal, *I Will Fight No More Forever.* University of Washington Press, Seattle, WA, 1963, pp. 107-108

3. O. O., Howard, *Nez Perce Joseph*, Boston: Lee and Shephard, 1881, p. 237

4. Beal, pp. 171-172

5. Gulick, p. 252

6. Beal, pp. 179-180

7. Beal, pp. 188-189

Chapter 12. Trails Across Montana

1. Merrill D. Beal, *I Will Fight No More Forever*, University of Washington Pres, Seattle, WA, 1963. P. 190

2. Bill Gulick, *Chief Joseph Country*, Caxton Printers, Ltd. Caldwell, ID, 1981, p. 256

Errata

This book has been reviewed by the Nez Perce Tribal Elders and by the Indian Education Specialist for the Montana Department of Education.

Please note that because there was no written Nez Perce language, many words have multiple written variations based on phonetic spellings. Every effort has been made to use one variation consistently throughout the text.

Page 9: The route taken by the Nez Perce going to Walla Walla was established by the author after studying several maps. The route actually taken probably lay farther north.

Page 14: The language used by Joseph after spearing a fish has been Americanized. The Nez Perce prayed for each animal, fish, or fowl that gave its life for their nourishment.

Page 15: The Nez Perce probably did not eat as a family unit but rather as a tribal group.

CPSIA information can be obtained at www.ICGtesting.com
Printed in the USA
BVOW01s1632120314

347449BV00001B/1/P